PENGUIN BOOKS

Sharp Family,

Muffin
BIBLE

Muffin

BIBLE

PENGUIN BOOKS

Hints for Making the Best Muffins

There are many useful tips for improving the taste and texture of your muffins, but they will all be to no avail if you overmix your batter — tough muffins can be a tough lesson. You should mix just enough to combine the wet and dry ingredients.

Preheat the oven to the required temperature and grease the muffin pans before you start. Also, have a read through the recipe before you begin so that you have all the chopping, grating and blending done before you start mixing the ingredients. The less time spent mixing things together, the better. Too much liquid in the mixture will result in soggy and flat muffins. Too little liquid and they'll end up hard and dry. Also, white flour instead of wholemeal will give you a lighter muffin.

The recipes in this book are intended to be cooked in standard 12-hole muffin pans. If you want to use jumbo or mini pans, use the oven temperature specified in the recipe, and increase or decrease cooking time. Your muffins are cooked when a skewer inserted into the centre of a muffin comes out clean.

Bake the muffins in the middle of the oven, and be adaptable with the temperature and timing of cooking – every oven behaves differently. The oven is too hot if the muffin tops are uneven and cracked, and it is too cool if the tops are pale and have not risen.

To reheat muffins, wrap them loosely in aluminium foil and put in the oven for 5–10 minutes at 125°C, or 15–20 minutes at 180°C if they are frozen.

Almond Chip Muffins

1¾ cups self-raising flour

2–3 tblsp caster sugar

1 tsp baking powder

½ tsp salt

1 egg

¾ cup milk

⅓ cup butter, melted

2 tsp grated lemon peel

½ tsp vanilla essence

¾ cup chopped, unblanched almonds

- In large bowl, sift together flour, sugar, baking powder and salt.

- In small bowl, combine egg, milk, melted butter, grated lemon peel, vanilla and almonds.

- Add to flour mixture. With a fork, stir briskly until all dry ingredients are moistened. Batter should look lumpy.

- Three-quarters fill greased muffin pans and bake at 200°C for 20–25 minutes or until golden brown.

Almond Poppy Seed Muffins

1 egg

¾ tsp salt

⅓ cup sugar

¼ cup oil

1 cup milk

2 cups flour

1 tblsp baking powder

¾ cup chopped almonds

⅓ cup poppy seeds

- Preheat oven to 200°C.

- Beat egg, salt and sugar until light and fluffy. Add oil in a stream and continue beating. Beat in milk.

- Sift flour and baking powder together several times and add to batter, stirring until just mixed. Add nuts and poppy seeds.

- Bake in greased muffin pans for 20 – 25 minutes.

Anzac Muffins

1 tsp baking soda

¾ cup warm milk

50g butter, melted

2 tblsp golden syrup

⅔ cup brown sugar

½ cup desiccated coconut

1 tsp baking powder

½ cup rolled oats

1 egg

2 cups flour

- Dissolve baking soda in milk, then add butter, golden syrup and brown sugar and mix well.

- Add remaining ingredients and stir until just combined.

- Three-quarters fill well-greased muffin pans and bake at 190°C for 15–20 minutes.

Apple Muffins

¹⁄₃ cup vegetable oil

¾ cup firmly packed brown sugar

1 tblsp liquid honey

2 eggs, lightly beaten

1 cup grated apple

½ cup apple juice

1½ cups All-bran

1 cup wholemeal flour

½ cup plain flour

1½ tsp baking powder

½ cup buttermilk

- Mix oil, brown sugar and honey. Add lightly beaten eggs and beat until thoroughly combined.

- Add grated apple and apple juice. Stir in All-bran.

- Sift dry ingredients. Stir into egg mixture with buttermilk until just combined.

- Three-quarters fill greased muffin pans and bake at 220°C for 15 minutes or until firm.

Apple Muffins with Maple Glaze

1⅓ cups flour

1 cup oats – quick or old-fashioned

½ cup sugar

1 tblsp baking powder

2 tsp ground cinnamon

½ cup milk

⅓ cup butter, melted

¼ cup maple syrup

2 egg whites, lightly beaten

1 cup chopped apple

toasted pecan halves

GLAZE

¼ cup icing sugar

1½ tblsp maple syrup

- Preheat oven to 200°C.

- Mix flour, oats, sugar, baking powder and cinnamon.

- Mix milk, butter, syrup and egg whites.

- Mix wet and dry ingredients until just blended. Gently stir in apple.

- Three-quarters fill muffin pans. Top each with a pecan half. Bake 20–25 minutes.

- Let stand a few minutes then remove from pans. Cool about 10 minutes.

- Mix together icing sugar and maple syrup. Leave muffins sitting on cooling rack under which you have placed sheets of waxed paper. Drizzle over glaze.

Apple, Date & Bran Muffins

2 eggs

½ cup brown sugar

¼ cup oil

2 cups skim milk

1 cup chopped dates

1 cup raisins

1 cup grated green apple

½ tsp cinnamon

1 cup bran

2 cups flour

½ cup wheatgerm

2 tsp baking soda

2 tsp baking powder

- Beat eggs lightly. Add sugar, oil, milk, dates and raisins, and stir to mix.

- Combine rest of ingredients and stir in egg mixture.

- Cover and chill for at least one hour.

- Three-quarters fill greased muffin pans and bake at 190°C for 20 minutes or until firm.

Apple-Nut Muffins

1 egg

⅔ cup apple juice or milk

½ cup oil

1 tsp vanilla essence

2 cups flour

¼ cup sugar

¼ cup brown sugar, packed

1 tblsp baking powder

½ tsp salt

½ cup chopped nuts

1 chopped apple

cinnamon sugar

- In bowl, beat egg with juice, oil and vanilla.

- Stir in flour, sugars, baking powder and salt until just moistened.

- Stir in nuts and apple.

- Three-quarters fill prepared muffin pans (greased or paper-lined). Sprinkle with cinnamon sugar (1 tsp cinnamon and 2 tblsp sugar mixed together).

- Bake at 200°C for 20 minutes or until golden brown.

Apricot & Almond Muffins

1 cup dried apricots

2 cups flour

1 egg

¾ cup milk

75g butter, melted

1 tblsp baking powder

½ cup sugar

70g almond slivers

- Cover apricots with water and bring to the boil.

- Leave to cool for at least one hour then drain, chop and transfer to a bowl.

- Add remaining ingredients and mix until just combined.

- Spoon into well-greased muffin pans and bake at 180°C for 15 minutes.

Apricot & Lemon Muffins

1 cup flour

½ tsp salt

1 tsp baking powder

1½ cups bran

¼ cup sugar

½ cup chopped apricots, dried or fresh

2 tsp grated lemon rind

½ tsp baking soda

1 cup milk

1 egg

1 tblsp butter, melted

1 tblsp golden syrup

- Sift flour, salt and baking powder.

- Stir in bran, sugar, chopped apricots and grated lemon rind. Make a well in centre of dry ingredients.

- Dissolve baking soda in milk. Beat egg lightly.

- Combine milk, melted butter, egg and golden syrup, and pour onto dry ingredients. Stir to just combine.

- Three-quarters fill greased muffin pans and bake at 200°C for 10–15 minutes or until firm.

Apricot & Walnut Muffins

12 dried apricots

2 tblsp brandy

2 cups flour

1 tblsp baking powder

½ cup sugar

½ cup chopped walnuts

1 egg

½ cup milk

50g butter, melted

- Cook apricots in brandy for five minutes and then roughly chop.

- Sift flour and baking powder and stir in sugar, chopped apricots and chopped walnuts.

- Combine egg and milk and add melted butter.

- Make a well in centre of dry ingredients and pour in milk and butter. Stir quickly until just combined.

- Three-quarters fill greased muffin pans and bake at 200°C for 15–20 minutes.

Artichoke Heart with Bacon & Garlic Muffins

¾ cup fresh breadcrumbs

1 clove crushed garlic

2 tblsp butter

1 egg, beaten

1 cup flour

¼ tsp salt

1 tblsp baking powder

½ cup grated cheese

1 cup artichoke hearts, quartered

2 rashers bacon, cooked and chopped

- Fry breadcrumbs and garlic in butter until crisp.

- Make egg up to 1 cup with water and mix with flour, salt, baking powder, cheese, artichokes and bacon until just combined.

- Three-quarters fill well-greased muffin pans and sprinkle with fried breadcrumbs.

- Bake at 200°C for 12–15 minutes.

Bacon & Cheese Muffins

1 cup flour

½ tsp salt

1 tsp baking powder

1½ cups bran

¼ cup sugar

½ tsp baking soda

1½ cups milk

1 egg

1 tblsp butter, melted

1 tblsp golden syrup

3 rashers cooked bacon

1 cup grated tasty cheese

- Sift flour, salt and baking powder. Stir in bran and sugar, and make a well in the centre.

- Dissolve baking soda in milk. Beat egg lightly.

- Combine milk, melted butter, egg and golden syrup.

- Add chopped bacon and cheese to dry ingredients, then pour in milk mixture. Stir until just combined.

- Three-quarters fill greased muffin pans and bake at 200°C for 10–15 minutes.

Bacon & Tomato Muffins

2 cups flour

1 tblsp baking powder

4 rashers bacon

2 tomatoes

2 tblsp tomato paste

1 egg

¾ cup milk

50g butter, melted

- Sift flour and baking powder.

- Cut rind off bacon and chop flesh.

- Skin and de-seed tomatoes, and chop roughly.

- Mix bacon, tomatoes, tomato paste, egg and milk together.

- Pour tomato mixture and melted butter into dry ingredients. Stir until just combined.

- Three-quarters fill greased muffin pans and bake at 200°C for 15–20 minutes.

Baileys, Cream Cheese & Chocolate Muffins

90g cream cheese

1½ tblsp Baileys Irish Cream

1 egg

¾ cup milk

⅓ cup water

50g butter, melted

100g chocolate, grated

1½ cups flour

2 tsp baking powder

½ tsp salt

3 tblsp cocoa

½ cup sugar

- Beat cream cheese until smooth, add Baileys and beat again.

- In separate bowl whisk egg, milk, water and butter, then add chocolate.

- Sift remaining dry ingredients into egg mixture and stir until just combined.

- One-third fill well-greased muffin pans with muffin mixture, make a hollow in centre, and fill with 1 teaspoon cream cheese mixture.

- Top up to three-quarters full with remaining muffin mixture.

- Bake at 190°C for 20 minutes.

Banana Choc Chip Muffins

1½ cups self-raising flour

⅓ cup caster sugar

60g butter

⅔ cup mashed banana

½ cup chocolate chips

1 egg

½ cup milk

FILLING

sliced banana

whipped cream

• In large bowl rub together flour, sugar and butter until mixture resembles fine breadcrumbs.

• Stir in mashed banana, chocolate chips, egg and milk to combine.

• Spoon mixture into prepared muffin pans and bake at 190°C for 20 minutes.

• Fold sliced banana into whipped cream and use to fill muffins.

Banana & Date Muffins

2½ cups oat bran
1½ cups wholemeal flour
6 tsp baking powder
2 tsp mixed spice
1 tsp cinnamon
500g finely chopped banana
100g finely chopped dates
½ cup apple juice concentrate
½ cup cold-pressed grapeseed oil
1 cup evaporated milk
3 egg whites

- Place oat bran in a bowl. Add sifted wholemeal flour, baking powder, mixed spice and cinnamon. Distribute flour and spices through oat bran with hands.

- Add banana and dates and toss well to break up and coat with flour.

- Combine apple juice concentrate, oil and milk, and combine with flour and oat mixture.

- Beat egg whites until soft, and gently fold through the mixture.

- Three-quarters fill greased muffin pans and bake at 180°C for 25–30 minutes.

Banana & Ginger Muffins

60g butter

2 tblsp sugar

1 egg

1 ripe banana, mashed

1 cup flour

1 tsp ground ginger

2 tblsp golden syrup

1 tsp baking soda

⅓ cup milk

FILLING

whipped cream

sugar

ground ginger

- Cream butter and sugar together, then add egg and mashed banana.
- Sift in flour and ginger.
- Dissolve syrup and baking soda in milk and add to mixture. Mix lightly.
- Spoon batter into prepared muffin pans and bake at 200°C for 15 minutes.
- Serve filled with fresh whipped cream flavoured with a little sugar and ground ginger.

Banana Lemon Muffins

110g unsalted butter

1¼ cups sugar

2 large eggs

1 cup mashed banana

2 tblsp lemon juice

1 tsp vanilla essence

2 cups flour

1 tsp baking soda

pinch of salt

¾ cup buttermilk (or use yoghurt or full cream milk)

- Grease muffin pans.

- Cream the butter and sugar until light and fluffy.

- Beat in eggs, one at a time.

- Whip in banana, lemon juice and vanilla.

- Sift flour, baking soda and salt together. Stir into banana mixture alternately with the buttermilk.

- Bake at 180°C for 20 minutes.

Banana Wholemeal Muffins

2 ripe bananas

1 egg

75g butter, melted

½ tsp baking soda

½ cup hot milk

1½ cups wholemeal flour

2 tsp baking powder

¼ tsp ground cinnamon

¼ tsp ground nutmeg

½ cup brown sugar

½ cup sultanas

- Mash bananas and add egg, butter and baking soda dissolved in milk.

- Add remaining ingredients and mix until just combined.

- Three-quarters fill well-greased muffin pans and bake at 200°C for 15–20 minutes.

Best Blueberry Muffins

2 cups flour

1 tblsp baking powder

2 tsp custard powder

1 cup sugar

¾ cup blueberries
(or blackcurrants)

2 eggs

¾ cup milk

¾ cup oil

icing sugar for dusting

- Sift flour, baking powder and custard powder into a bowl. Add sugar and blueberries.

- In separate bowl mix together eggs, milk and oil.

- Add milk mixture to dry ingredients and combine.

- Spoon batter into prepared muffin pans and bake at 190°C for 15–20 minutes.

- Serve dusted with icing sugar.

Black Bottom Muffins

1¼ cups flour

¾ cup sugar

⅓ cup cocoa

½ tsp baking soda

¼ tsp salt

⅔ cup buttermilk

¼ cup oil

60g butter, melted and cooled slightly

1 egg

1 tsp vanilla essence

⅓ cup chocolate chips

TOPPING

200g cream cheese

¼ cup sugar

1 egg

⅛ tsp almond essence

¼ cup toasted slivered almonds

- In large bowl mix together flour, sugar, cocoa, baking soda and salt.

- In separate bowl mix together buttermilk, oil, butter, egg and vanilla until well combined.

- Make a well in centre of dry ingredients and add buttermilk mixture. Stir to combine, then mix in chocolate chips.

- Spoon batter into prepared muffin pans, then cover with topping. Bake at 190°C for 20 minutes.

- To make topping, combine cream cheese, sugar, egg and almond essence, then fold in almonds.

Black Forest Muffins

1 egg

150g dark chocolate melted in
1 cup boiling water

75g butter, softened

2 cups flour

2 tsp baking powder

1 tblsp cocoa

½ cup caster sugar

1 cup glacé cherries

FILLING

100g chocolate, melted

100g sour cream

1½ cups icing sugar

raspberry jam

- Mix muffin ingredients together until just combined.

- Three-quarters fill well-greased muffin pans and bake at 180°C for 15–20 minutes. Leave to cool.

- To make filling, mix chocolate, sour cream and icing sugar.

- Remove muffins from pans, make a diagonal cut into each, spread cuts thinly with raspberry jam and fill with icing.

Black & White Muffins

50g butter, softened

½ cup caster sugar

1 egg

1 cup milk

2 cups flour

2 tsp baking powder

80g white chocolate, chopped

1 tblsp cocoa

80g dark chocolate, chopped

- Cream butter and sugar until fluffy.

- Add egg and milk, then mix in flour and baking powder until just combined.

- Divide mixture between two bowls. Add white chocolate to one, and to the other add cocoa and dark chocolate.

- Line muffin pans with paper cases and half fill each with white mixture, then top with dark mixture.

- Bake at 190°C for 20 minutes.

Blackberry Muffins

¾ cup natural yoghurt

½ cup water

2 eggs

2 cups blackberries
(fresh, frozen or canned)

3 cups flour

1 tblsp baking powder

½ tsp baking soda

1½ cups sugar

icing sugar for dusting

- If using canned blackberries, reserve juice from berries and use ½ cup of this in place of water.

- Mix yoghurt, water or juice and eggs.

- Add remaining ingredients and mix until just combined.

- Spoon into well-greased muffin pans and bake at 180°C for 15–20 minutes.

- Dust with icing sugar just before serving.

Blueberry Fat-Free Muffins

1¾ cups rolled oats

½ cup oat bran

¾ tsp baking soda

½ tsp cinnamon

¾ cup unsweetened apple sauce

½ cup honey

1 tsp vanilla essence

½ cup non-fat milk

3 egg whites, lightly beaten

1 cup blueberries

- Pulse rolled oats and oat bran in food processor for 10 seconds. Reserve 2 tblsp oat mixture.

- In medium bowl, combine remaining oat mixture, baking soda and cinnamon. Mix well and set aside.

- In small bowl, combine apple sauce, honey, vanilla and milk. Pour into oat mixture. Stir until just blended.

- Gently mix in egg whites.

- Dust well-drained blueberries with 2 tblsp reserved oat mixture. Gently fold the blueberries into batter.

- Divide mixture evenly into greased muffin pans and bake at 180°C for 20–25 minutes.

Blueberry Maple Muffins

1 cup bran flakes, lightly crushed

1 cup sour cream

1 cup maple syrup

2 eggs

2 cups flour

2 tsp baking soda

1 cup blueberries

1 cup walnuts, chopped

- The night before baking, combine bran flakes with sour cream and maple syrup and refrigerate overnight.

- Grease muffin pans or line with paper cases.

- Beat eggs until frothy and blend into bran flake mixture.

- Combine flour with baking soda and stir into batter until blended. Fold in blueberries.

- Spoon batter into prepared pans, then sprinkle walnuts evenly over muffins. Bake at 200°C for 15–20 minutes.

Brazil Nut & Fruit Muffins

2 cups flour

⅔ cup brown sugar, packed

2 tsp baking powder

½ tsp salt

1 cup chopped dried apricots

¾ cup boiling water

½ cup oil

½ cup mashed banana

1 egg

1 tsp vanilla essence

1 cup chopped brazil nuts

- In large bowl mix together flour, brown sugar, baking powder and salt.

- In separate bowl combine apricots and boiling water and allow to soak for five minutes.

- Stir oil, banana, egg and vanilla into apricots.

- Make a well in centre of dry ingredients and add apricot mixture. Stir to combine, then fold in nuts.

- Spoon batter into prepared muffin pans and bake at 200°C for 16–20 minutes.

- Serve with butter while still warm.

Cappuccino Chip Muffins

2 cups flour

¾ cup sugar

2½ tsp baking powder

2 tsp instant coffee

½ tsp salt

½ tsp ground cinnamon

1 cup milk

125g butter, melted and cooled slightly

1 egg

1 tsp vanilla essence

¾ cup chocolate chips

grated chocolate for sprinkling

FILLING

100g cream cheese

1 tblsp sugar

½ tsp vanilla essence

½ tsp coffee powder

- In large bowl mix together flour, sugar, baking powder, coffee, salt and cinnamon.

- In separate bowl mix together milk, butter, egg and vanilla.

- Make a well in centre of dry ingredients and add milk mixture. Stir to combine, then fold in chocolate chips.

- Spoon batter into prepared muffin tins and bake at 190°C for 15–20 minutes.

- Cut in half, spread with filling and sprinkle with grated chocolate.

- To make filling, cream ingredients together.

Caraway & Cheese Muffins

2 cups flour

1 tblsp baking powder

¼ tsp salt

1 tsp dried mustard

1 cup grated cheese

1 tblsp caraway seeds

1 egg

¾ cup milk

50g butter, melted

- Sift flour, baking powder and salt.

- Stir in mustard, grated cheese and caraway seeds.

- Combine egg and milk. Stir melted butter, egg and milk into dry ingredients until just combined.

- Three-quarters fill greased muffin pans and bake at 200°C for 15–20 minutes.

Cardamom Muffins

1½ cups self-raising flour

pinch salt

1 tsp ground cardamom

¼ cup sugar

1 egg

50g butter, melted

⅓ cup sour cream

- Sift flour, salt and cardamom and stir in sugar.

- Beat egg, melted butter and sour cream.

- Pour onto dry ingredients and mix until just combined.

- Three-quarters fill greased muffin pans and bake at 200°C for 15–20 minutes.

Carrot, Bacon & Parsley Muffins

2 cups flour

4 tsp baking powder

1 cup grated cheese

1 grated onion

1 cup grated carrot

chopped parsley

2 tblsp bacon bits

1 egg

1 large tblsp butter, melted

1 cup milk

- Sift flour and baking powder.

- Add cheese, onion, carrot, parsley and bacon bits.

- Beat egg, then add melted butter and milk. Mix until just combined.

- Three-quarters fill greased muffin pans and bake at 200°C for 15–20 minutes.

Carrot Cake Muffins

1¾ cups flour

⅔ cup firmly packed light brown sugar

1 tsp baking powder

½ tsp baking soda

½ tsp salt

1 tsp ground cinnamon

dash ground mace

½ cup crushed pineapple in juice

½ cup vegetable oil

1 egg, lightly beaten

1½ tsp vanilla essence

2 cups shredded carrot

½ cup raisins

- In large bowl, mix flour, brown sugar, baking powder, baking soda, salt, cinnamon and mace.

- In separate bowl, mix pineapple, oil, egg and vanilla until blended.

- Make a well in centre of dry ingredients, add pineapple mixture and stir to just combine.

- Stir in carrot and raisins.

- Spoon batter into prepared muffin pans and bake at 200°C for 15–20 minutes.

Carrot & Ginger Muffins

2 cups flour

1 tblsp baking powder

¼ tsp ground ginger

¼ cup brown sugar

¾ cup grated carrot

¼ cup crystallized ginger

1 egg

¾ cup milk

50g butter, melted

- Sift flour, baking powder and ground ginger. Stir in sugar, carrot and crystallized ginger.

- Combine egg and milk, and add melted butter.

- Make a well in centre of dry ingredients and pour in milk and butter. Stir quickly until just combined.

- Three-quarters fill greased muffin pans and bake at 200°C for 20 minutes.

Cheese Muffins

2 cups flour

3 tsp baking powder

¼ tsp salt

½ tsp dry mustard

freshly ground black pepper

2 cups grated tasty cheese

2 eggs

1 cup milk

- Sift flour, baking powder, salt, mustard and freshly ground pepper.

- Add grated cheese.

- Lightly beat eggs and milk together. Add eggs and milk to dry ingredients and mix together lightly until just combined.

- Three-quarters fill greased muffin pans and bake at 200°C for 10–15 minutes or until golden brown.

Cheese & Chive Muffins

1 egg

¾ cup water

1 cup self-raising flour

½ tsp salt

1½ cups grated cheese

1 tblsp fresh chives

coarse sea salt (optional)

- Mix all ingredients together until just combined.

- Spoon into well-greased muffin pans and sprinkle with sea salt.

- Bake at 190°C for 15 minutes.

Cheese & Onion Muffins

½ cup chopped onion
1 tblsp melted butter
1 egg, lightly beaten
½ cup milk
1½ cups self-raising flour
pinch salt
1 level tblsp butter
1 cup grated tasty cheese
1 tblsp poppy seeds
1 tblsp melted butter for drizzling

- Cook onions in one tablespoon of melted butter until lightly brown.

- Mix beaten egg and milk together.

- Sift flour and salt. Rub in one tablespoon of butter.

- Mix dry ingredients with egg and milk to make a light scone batter.

- Add onions and half the cheese.

- Place small rounds in greased muffin pans and sprinkle with remaining grated cheese and poppy seeds. Drizzle melted butter over top of muffins.

- Bake at 220°C for 15 minutes.

Cheese & Tomato Layer Muffins

1 egg

¾ cup water

2 cups self-raising flour

½ tsp salt

1½ cups grated cheddar

¾ cup tomato cooking sauce

- Combine all ingredients except tomato cooking sauce.

- Half fill prepared muffin pans with mixture.

- Put up to 2 teaspoons sauce in the middle of each muffin. Take care that sauce stays mostly in the middle. If there is too much sauce, muffins will come apart when removed from pans.

- Cover each muffin with remaining mixture until pans are three-quarters full. Bake at 200°C for 12–15 minutes.

Cherry Muffins

2 cups, plus 2 tblsp, flour

1 cup sugar

2 tsp baking powder

¼ tsp salt

2 eggs, beaten

½ cup milk

½ cup butter or margarine, melted

1 tsp almond essence

2 cups fresh or canned pitted red cherries, drained

TOPPING

1–2 tblsp sugar

¼ tsp ground nutmeg

1–2 tblsp sliced almonds

- In mixing bowl, stir together flour, sugar, baking powder and salt. Make a well in centre and set aside.

- In another bowl, combine eggs, milk, butter and essence.

- Add to flour mixture all at once; stir until just moistened. Gently fold in cherries.

- Spoon into well-greased muffin pans.

- Combine topping ingredients and sprinkle over batter.

- Bake at 190°C for 20–25 minutes.

Cherry & Walnut Muffins

2 cups flour

⅓ cup caster sugar

3 tsp baking powder

¼ cup chopped glacé cherries

⅓ cup chopped walnuts

1 egg

1 cup milk

¼ cup butter, melted

1 tsp vanilla essence

- Sift flour, sugar and baking powder, then add cherries and walnuts.

- Beat together egg, milk, melted butter and vanilla.

- Add to dry ingredients and mix gently until just combined.

- Three-quarters fill greased muffin pans and bake at 200°C for 15–20 minutes.

Chilli Corn Muffins

1 finely chopped chilli or
1 tsp chilli powder

1 finely chopped small onion

¼ cup oil

1½ cups All-bran

1½ cups skim milk

2 egg whites

1⅔ cups self-raising flour

1 × 325g can corn kernels, drained

½ cup grated tasty cheese

1 egg white, stiffly beaten

- Sauté chilli and onion in one tablespoon of oil until onion is tender. Cool.

- Place All-bran and milk in a bowl and stand for five minutes to soften.

- Stir in chilli mixture, remaining oil and two egg whites. Add flour, corn and ¼ cup cheese.

- Finally, fold in remaining stiffly beaten egg white.

- Three-quarters fill greased muffin pans and sprinkle each muffin with a little of the remaining cheese.

- Bake at 190°C for 25–30 minutes.

Chocolate Muffins

150g fine cornmeal

⅓ cup self-raising flour

2 tblsp cocoa

1 tblsp baking powder

pinch of salt

⅓ cup dark brown sugar

60g butter, melted

⅔ cup sour cream

1 egg

2 tblsp strong black coffee

50g dark chocolate, broken into 12 pieces

cocoa for dusting

- Sift cornmeal, flour, cocoa, baking powder and salt into a bowl.

- Add brown sugar, then stir in butter, sour cream, egg and coffee.

- Spoon half the batter into prepared muffin pans.

- Place a piece of chocolate in each pan, then cover with remaining batter.

- Bake at 200°C for 20 minutes.

- Dust with cocoa before serving.

Chocolate Big Chip Muffins

2 cups flour

⅓ cup brown sugar,
firmly packed

⅓ cup sugar

2 tsp baking powder

½ tsp salt

⅔ cup milk

2 eggs

125g butter, melted and
cooled slightly

1 tsp vanilla essence

2 cups large chocolate chips
or chunks

½ cup chopped pecans

- In large bowl mix together flour, sugars, baking powder and salt.

- In separate bowl mix together milk, eggs, butter and vanilla.

- Make a well in centre of dry ingredients and add milk mixture. Stir to combine, then fold in chocolate chips and pecans.

- Spoon batter into prepared muffin pans and bake at 200°C for 15–20 minutes.

VARIATION: Serve topped with chocolate icing and sprinkled with chocolate chips and pecans.

Chocolate Bourbon Muffins

¾ cup flour

½ tsp baking soda

¼ tsp salt

125g butter, softened

½ cup sugar

50g chocolate, melted and
cooled slightly

1 egg

1 tblsp bourbon

1 tsp vanilla essence

½ cup chocolate chips

½ cup chopped pecans

icing sugar or cocoa for dusting

- Mix together flour, baking soda and salt.

- In separate bowl cream butter and sugar until light and fluffy, then beat in chocolate, egg, bourbon and vanilla.

- Add dry ingredients and combine, then fold in chocolate chips and pecans.

- Spoon batter into prepared muffin pans and bake at 200°C for 15–20 minutes.

- Serve dusted with icing sugar or cocoa.

Chocolate Caramel Muffins

1 egg

75g soft butter

150g dark chocolate melted in
1 cup boiling water

2 cups flour

2 tsp baking powder

1 tblsp cocoa

½ cup caster sugar

FILLING

½ × 400g can sweetened
condensed milk

1½ tsp butter

1 tblsp golden syrup

- Mix all muffin ingredients together until just combined.

- Three-quarters fill well-greased muffin pans and bake at 180°C for 15–20 minutes. Leave to cool.

- To make filling, boil ingredients, stirring every 30 seconds, until they thicken into caramel. Take care as this mixture changes quickly.

- Remove muffins from pans, make a diagonal cut into each and fill with caramel.

Chocolate Cherry Brandy Muffins

1 egg

150g dark chocolate, melted in
1 cup boiling water

75g butter, softened

2 cups flour

2 tsp baking powder

1 tblsp cocoa

½ cup caster sugar

1 cup glacé cherries mixed with
¼ cup brandy

- Mix all ingredients together until just combined.

- Three-quarters fill prepared muffin pans and bake at 180°C for 15–20 minutes.

Chocolate Raspberry Muffins

1 × 425g can raspberries in syrup

2 cups self-raising flour

½ cup sugar

½ cup chocolate chips

1 egg

60g butter, melted and cooled slightly

¾ cup buttermilk

FILLING

1 × 300ml carton cream

2 tblsp cocoa

2 tblsp icing sugar

2 tblsp raspberry jam

- Put undrained raspberries in a saucepan and bring to boil. Simmer for 12 minutes, then allow to cool.

- In large bowl mix together flour, sugar and chocolate chips.

- In separate bowl mix together egg, butter and buttermilk.

- Make a well in centre of dry ingredients and add buttermilk mixture. Stir to combine, then fold in raspberry mixture.

- Spoon into prepared muffin pans and bake at 190°C for 15 minutes.

- To serve, split and add filling.

- To make filling, whip cream, cocoa and icing sugar together, then fold in jam.

Christmas Morning
Cranberry Muffins

1 cup cranberries

½ cup sugar

1½ cups flour

2 tsp baking powder

1 tsp salt

½ tsp ground cinnamon

¼ tsp ground allspice

¼ tsp ground nutmeg

1 egg, beaten

¼ tsp grated orange rind

¾ cup orange juice

75g butter, melted and cooled slightly

¼ cup chopped nuts

- Chop cranberries coarsely and sprinkle with half the sugar. Set aside.

- In large bowl mix together remaining sugar, flour, baking powder, salt and spices.

- In separate bowl mix together egg, orange rind, orange juice and butter.

- Make a well in centre of dry ingredients and add orange mixture. Stir to moisten, then fold in cranberries and chopped nuts.

- Spoon batter into prepared muffin pans and bake at 190°C for 15–20 minutes.

Christmas Muffins

2½ cups sugar

4 cups flour

4 tsp cinnamon

4 tsp baking soda

1 tsp salt

1 cup raisins, plumped in brandy and drained

1 cup desiccated coconut

4 cups grated carrot

2 cups grated apple

1 cup pecans or walnuts, roughly chopped

6 eggs

2 cups vegetable oil

1 tsp vanilla essence

icing sugar for dusting

• Sift dry ingredients into large bowl.

• Lightly dust raisins with flour.

• Add coconut, carrot, apple and nuts, and stir well.

• Add eggs, oil and vanilla. Stir until combined.

• Spoon into deep muffin pans and bake at 190°C for 20 minutes.

• Serve dusted with icing sugar.

• Quantities can be halved.

Cinnamon Sugar Muffins

2 tsp ground cinnamon

⅔ cup sugar

2 cups self-raising flour

¾ cup water

1 egg

2 tblsp golden syrup

- Mix cinnamon and sugar together. Reserve one-third for topping and two-thirds for muffin centres.

- Mix remaining ingredients together until just combined.

- One-third fill well-greased muffin pans with mixture and sprinkle with two-thirds of the cinnamon sugar.

- Fill pans with remaining mixture and sprinkle with the rest of the cinnamon sugar.

- Bake at 200°C for 15 minutes.

Coconut Pineapple Muffins

2 cups flour

1 tblsp baking powder

½ tsp salt

½ cup sugar

½ cup coconut

1 egg

¼ cup oil

⅓ cup milk

1 tsp vanilla essence

1 × 225g can crushed pineapple, drained

½ cup slivered almonds

- In large bowl mix together flour, baking powder, salt, sugar and coconut.

- In separate bowl mix together egg, oil, milk, vanilla and pineapple.

- Add to dry ingredients and stir until just moistened.

- Spoon batter into prepared muffin pans and sprinkle over slivered almonds.

- Bake at 200°C for 20 minutes.

Coffee Walnut Muffins

1 tblsp instant coffee

½ cup hot water

1 cup milk or cream

1 egg, beaten

½ cup oil

2 cups flour

⅓ cup sugar

3 tsp baking powder

1 tsp salt

½ cup chopped walnuts

icing sugar for dusting

- Dissolve coffee in hot water. Add milk or cream, egg and oil.

- In large bowl mix together flour, sugar, baking powder and salt, then add walnuts.

- Add milk mixture to dry ingredients and stir.

- Spoon batter into prepared muffin pans and bake at 200°C for 15–20 minutes.

- Serve dusted with icing sugar.

Corn & Bacon Muffins

1 egg

2 cups flour

½ tsp salt

1 tblsp baking powder

1 cup creamed corn

1 cup grated cheese

2 rashers bacon, cooked and chopped

• Make egg up to ¾ cup with water.

• Add remaining ingredients and mix until just combined.

• Spoon into prepared muffin pans and bake at 200°C for 15–20 minutes.

Corn Muffins with Sun-Dried Tomatoes

60g coarse cornmeal

70g plain flour

2 tsp caster sugar

1½ tsp baking powder

¼ tsp salt

1 small egg

100ml milk

1 tblsp corn oil

25g sun-dried tomatoes in oil, drained and finely chopped

- Stir all dry ingredients in a bowl.

- Beat egg with milk and oil and gently mix into flour.

- Fold chopped sun-dried tomatoes into batter.

- Spoon into greased muffin pans.

- Bake at 220°C for 12 minutes.

- By using coarse-ground cornmeal or polenta, the muffins have a lovely crunchy texture.

VARIATION: You could vary the flavour by adding chopped chilli, olives, garlic, etc. to the muffin mix in place of sun-dried tomatoes.

Corn & Tomato Muffins

¾ cup cornmeal

½ cup white flour

1 tblsp granulated sugar

3 tsp baking powder

¼ tsp salt

⅔ cup skim milk

1 egg white, lightly beaten

½ cup plum tomatoes, seeded and diced

1 tblsp fresh basil, minced

fresh oregano

- Spray muffin pans with vegetable oil spray.

- In medium bowl, combine cornmeal, flour, sugar, baking powder and salt. Set aside.

- In small bowl, combine milk, egg white, tomato and herbs. Pour into flour mixture, stirring until just combined.

- Spoon into muffin pans and bake at 200°C for 20 minutes.

Cottage Cheese Muffins

2 cups flour

½ tsp salt

1 tsp dry mustard

2½ tsp baking powder

25g butter

1 egg

¾ cup milk

250g cottage cheese

¼ cup chopped parsley

1 small onion, finely chopped

¼ cup grated tasty cheese

¼ tsp paprika

- Sift flour, salt, mustard and baking powder. Rub in butter.

- Beat together egg and milk, then add cottage cheese, parsley and onion. Mix well.

- Stir liquid into dry ingredients until just combined.

- Three-quarters fill greased muffin pans, then sprinkle mixed grated cheese and paprika over muffins.

- Bake at 200°C for 20 minutes.

- Serve warm.

Cottage Cheese & Cheddar Muffins

1 egg

¾ cup water

1 cup cottage cheese

1 cup self-raising flour

1 tsp salt

1 cup grated tasty cheese

2 tblsp grated Parmesan cheese

- Mix together all ingredients except Parmesan until just combined.

- Spoon into well-greased muffin pans and sprinkle with Parmesan.

- Bake at 190°C for 12–15 minutes.

Cranberry & Apple Muffins

1½ cups flour

1 tsp baking soda

1 tsp cinnamon

¼ tsp salt

2 egg whites, whipped

¾ cup brown sugar, packed

¼ cup apple sauce

1 tsp vanilla essence

¾ cup apple, peeled and chopped finely

¾ cup cranberries, chopped

- Grease muffin pans and dust with flour.

- In mixing bowl, combine flour, baking soda, cinnamon and salt.

- In separate bowl, combine egg whites, brown sugar, apple sauce, vanilla, apple and cranberries.

- Mix dry ingredients with wet ingredients until just combined.

- Fill muffin pans three-quarters full.

- Bake at 180°C for 20–25 minutes, or until lightly browned.

Cream Cheese & Lemon Muffins

110g cream cheese

1½ cups flour

grated rind of 1 lemon

1 egg

½ cup, plus 1 tsp, oil

½ cup milk

⅔ cup sugar

1½ tsp baking powder

½ tsp salt

TOPPING

2 tblsp lemon juice (fresh)

1 tblsp sugar

- Cut cream cheese into small pieces, mix with 2 tablespoons flour and grate the lemon rind into the mixture.

- Add rest of ingredients.

- Mix until just combined and spoon into greased muffin pans.

- Bake at 190°C for 20–25 minutes.

- To make topping, mix to form lemon sugar. Sprinkle over warm muffins.

Date Muffins

2 tblsp butter

¼ cup brown sugar

2 eggs

1 cup milk

2 cups flour

1 tsp baking powder

pinch of salt

1 cup finely chopped dates

• Cream butter and sugar.

• Add eggs and milk, then sifted flour, baking powder and salt.

• Fold in finely chopped dates. Stir to just combine.

• Three-quarters fill greased muffin pans and bake at 200°C for 12–15 minutes.

Date & Orange Muffins

1 orange, peeled and quartered

½ cup orange juice

1 egg

100g butter, melted

1½ cups flour

1 tsp baking powder

¼ tsp salt

1 tsp baking soda

¾ cup sugar

½ cup chopped dates

- Place orange in food processor and process until pulp.

- Add orange juice, egg and melted butter, and combine.

- Sift flour, baking powder, salt, baking soda and sugar.

- Add mixture from processor to dry ingredients. Add chopped dates and mix until just combined.

- Three-quarters fill greased muffin pans and bake at 190°C for 15 minutes or until cooked.

Date & Walnut Muffins

1 tsp baking soda

1 cup chopped dates

¾ cup boiling water

2 eggs

1 cup brown sugar

1 tsp vanilla essence

1½ cups flour

½ tsp salt

2 tsp baking powder

½ cup roughly chopped walnuts

- Sprinkle baking soda over dates, pour over boiling water and leave to cool.

- Whisk eggs, sugar and vanilla and mix into cooled date mix.

- Add dry ingredients and mix until just combined.

- Spoon into well-greased muffin pans and bake at 180°C for 18 minutes.

Double Chocolate Muffins

¼ cup cocoa

¼ cup boiling water

3 cups self-raising flour

¾ cup sugar

1 cup chocolate chips

1 egg, beaten

1½ cups evaporated milk

125g butter, melted and cooled slightly

icing sugar or cocoa for dusting

- Mix cocoa and boiling water together to make a smooth paste. Allow to cool.

- Sift flour and sugar into a large bowl and add chocolate chips.

- In separate bowl mix together cocoa mixture, egg, evaporated milk and butter.

- Make a well in centre of dry ingredients and add milk mixture. Stir until just combined.

- Spoon batter into prepared muffin pans and bake at 190°C for 20 minutes.

- Serve dusted with icing sugar or cocoa.

Doughnut-Flavoured Muffins

1¾ cups flour

1½ tsp baking powder

½ tsp salt

¼ tsp ground cinnamon

½ tsp ground nutmeg

⅓ cup oil

¾ cup sugar

1 egg

¾ cup milk

TOPPING

½ cup melted butter

¾ cup sugar

1 tsp ground cinnamon

- In large bowl mix together flour, baking powder, salt and spices.

- In separate bowl mix together oil, sugar, egg and milk. Add oil mixture to dry ingredients and stir to combine.

- Spoon batter into prepared muffin pans and bake at 190°C for 20 minutes.

- Remove from pans while still warm and brush with melted butter, then sprinkle with sugar and cinnamon mixed together.

VARIATION: Half fill muffin pans with batter. Add 1 tsp raspberry jam in each pan and cover with rest of batter.

Extra-Fibre Muffins

1¼ cups flour

½ cup sugar

1 tblsp baking powder

2 cups All bran

1¼ cups skim milk

1 egg

¼ cup apple sauce

- Stir together flour, sugar and baking powder.

- In large mixing bowl combine cereal and milk. Let stand 5 minutes or until cereal softens.

- Add egg and apple sauce. Beat well.

- Add flour mixture, stirring until just combined.

- Three-quarters fill muffin pans and bake at 200°C for 20 minutes until lightly brown.

Fresh Fruit Muffins

2 cups flour

4 tsp baking powder

½ tsp salt

½ cup caster sugar

100g butter, melted and
cooled slightly

1 cup milk

1 egg

1–1½ cups chopped fresh fruit

1 cup chopped walnuts

1 tblsp sugar for sprinkling

½ tsp ground cinnamon
for sprinkling

- In large bowl mix together flour, baking powder, salt and sugar.

- In separate bowl mix together melted butter, milk and egg.

- Add milk mixture to dry ingredients, followed by prepared fruit and walnuts. Stir to combine.

- Spoon into prepared muffin pans and sprinkle with sugar and cinnamon mixed together.

- Bake at 200°C for 15 minutes.

- Split and serve with butter.

VARIATION: Serve with yoghurt mixed with the appropriate fruit. Also good with whipped cream.

Fresh Raspberry Muffins

2 cups flour

¾ tsp baking soda

¾ tsp cinnamon

¼ tsp freshly grated nutmeg

¼ tsp ground ginger

¼ tsp salt

1 cup sugar

2 large eggs

2 tsp vanilla essence

½ cup oil

4 tblsp melted butter, cooled

1 cup fresh raspberries

- Blend together flour, baking soda, cinnamon, nutmeg, ginger and salt in large mixing bowl.

- Whisk sugar and eggs in small bowl until light. Blend in vanilla, oil and butter.

- Make a large well in centre of dry ingredients, pour in egg-sugar mixture and combine the two mixtures quickly until batter is formed.

- Gently fold in raspberries.

- Spoon batter into prepared muffin pans, filling them two-thirds full.

- Bake at 200°C for 20–22 minutes.

Fruit Salad Muffins

2 eggs

1 × 400–450g can fruit salad in juice, drained (juice reserved)

¾ cup reserved juice

100g butter, melted

2 cups self-raising flour

½ cup sugar

- Mix all ingredients together until just combined.

- Spoon into well-greased muffin pans and bake at 180°C for 15–20 minutes.

Fruit Yoghurt Muffins

1 egg

¾ cup water

150g fruit-flavoured yoghurt

50g butter, melted

2 cups flour

1 tblsp baking powder

½ cup sugar

- Mix all ingredients until just combined.

- Three-quarters fill well-greased muffin pans and bake at 180°C for 15–20 minutes.

Fruity Muffins

75g butter

1 egg, beaten

1 cup milk

1–1½ cups fruit (peaches, pineapple, blueberries, apricots, strawberries) cut into small cubes

2 cups flour

4 tsp baking powder

½ tsp salt

½ cup caster sugar

1 tblsp sugar for sprinkling

½ tsp cinnamon for sprinkling

- Melt butter, add egg and milk and beat to combine.

- Add with fruit to sifted dry ingredients. Don't over mix.

- Spoon into greased muffin pans and sprinkle with sugar and cinnamon mixed together.

- Bake at 220°C for 15–20 minutes.

Fruity Bran Muffins

1¼ cups All-bran
¾ cup skim milk
1 egg
¼ cup oil
¼ cup raw sugar
1¾ cups self-raising flour
1 tsp cinnamon
⅔ cup mixed dried fruit
1 egg white
extra All-bran for topping

- Place All-bran and milk in bowl and let stand for five minutes to soften.

- Beat egg, oil and sugar together and add to All-bran.

- Sift flour and add to All-bran with cinnamon and mixed fruit. Mix until just combined.

- Fold in stiffly beaten egg white.

- Three-quarters fill greased muffin pans and sprinkle each muffin with some extra All-bran.

- Bake at 190°C for 25–30 minutes or until cooked.

Fudge-Filled Peanut Butter Muffins

½ cup chocolate chips

1 tblsp unsalted butter

1⅔ cups flour

1 tblsp baking powder

½ cup brown sugar, firmly packed

¼ tsp salt

¾ cup milk

½ cup peanut butter

⅓ cup oil

1 egg, beaten

1½ tsp vanilla essence

½ cup chopped salted peanuts

- In small saucepan heat chocolate chips and butter until melted. Reserve.

- In large bowl mix together flour, baking powder, sugar and salt.

- In separate bowl mix together milk, peanut butter, oil, egg and vanilla until well combined.

- Make a well in centre of dry ingredients and add milk mixture. Stir to combine.

- Spoon half the batter into prepared muffin pans. Put a spoonful of melted chocolate mixture on top, making sure it does not touch the sides. Cover with remaining batter.

- Sprinkle over chopped peanuts and bake at 200°C for 15–20 minutes.

Garden Herb Muffins

2 cups flour

1 tblsp granulated sugar

2 tsp baking powder

1 tsp garlic powder

1 tsp dry mustard

½ tsp salt

2 egg whites, lightly beaten

1 cup skim milk

½ cup grated carrot

¼ cup chopped green onion

2 tblsp olive oil

2 tblsp non-fat plain yoghurt

- Into large bowl, sift together flour and the next five dry ingredients.

- In small mixing bowl, combine egg and remaining ingredients.

- Blend egg mixture gently into flour mixture.

- Spoon batter into prepared muffin pans.

- Bake at 190°C for 18–20 minutes.

Ginger Muffins

1 cup milk

50g butter

1 tblsp golden syrup

1 tsp baking soda

1 egg, lightly beaten

1 cup oat bran

½ cup sugar

2 tblsp chopped crystallized ginger

1 tsp ground ginger

1 cup flour

½ cup rolled oats

½ tsp salt

- Heat milk, butter and golden syrup until butter melts. Add baking soda and egg.

- In bowl, mix oat bran, sugar, crystallized and ground ginger, flour, rolled oats and salt.

- Add milk mixture and mix until only just combined.

- Three-quarters fill greased muffin pans and bake at 200°C for 10–15 minutes.

Ginger Pear Muffins

2 cups flour

½ cup brown sugar, firmly packed

1 tsp baking soda

½ tsp salt

2 tsp ground ginger

1 tsp ground cinnamon

pinch each of ground nutmeg, ground cloves

1 cup natural yoghurt

½ cup oil

3 tblsp molasses

1 egg, beaten

1½ cups diced pears

½ cup raisins

¼ cup chopped walnuts

- In large bowl mix together flour, brown sugar, baking soda, salt and spices.

- In separate bowl mix together yoghurt, oil, molasses and egg.

- Make a well in centre of dry ingredients and add yoghurt mixture. Stir to combine, then fold in pears, raisins and walnuts.

- Spoon batter into prepared muffin pans and bake at 200°C for 20 minutes. Serve warm with butter.

VARIATION: Top with ginger icing, made from 1½ cups icing sugar, 1 tsp ground ginger, 1 tblsp butter and boiling water to mix.

Ginger Pineapple Muffins

2 eggs

1 cup milk

100g butter, melted

1 × 440g can crushed pineapple, drained

1 cup white flour

1 cup wholemeal flour

1 tblsp baking powder

½ cup bran

2 tsp ground ginger

½ cup brown sugar

- Mix all ingredients together until just combined.

- Three-quarters fill greased muffin pans and bake at 180°C for 15–20 minutes.

HINT: Up to half the milk can be replaced by the liquid from the pineapple if it is in juice. Don't use if it is syrup.

Gingerbread Lemon-Iced Muffins

1¼ cups flour

½ cup wholemeal flour

½ cup brown sugar, firmly packed

1 tsp baking soda

¼ tsp salt

2 tsp ground ginger

1 tsp ground cinnamon

⅛ tsp ground cloves

⅛ tsp ground nutmeg

¾ cup buttermilk

½ cup oil

2 eggs, beaten

¼ cup molasses

1 cup currants

GLAZE

¾ cup icing sugar

2 tsp lemon juice

- In large bowl mix together flours, sugar, baking soda, salt and spices.

- In separate bowl mix together buttermilk, oil, eggs and molasses.

- Make a well in centre of dry ingredients and add buttermilk mixture. Stir to combine, then fold in currants.

- Spoon batter into prepared muffin pans and bake at 200°C for 15–20 minutes.

- To serve, beat icing sugar and lemon juice and drizzle over muffins.

Goat Cheese & Pesto Muffins

½ cup pesto

¾ cup water

1 egg

2 cups flour

½ tsp salt

1 tblsp baking powder

100g goat cheese, crumbled or cubed

1 cup grated cheddar

- Stir pesto into water, then mix with remaining ingredients until just combined.

- Spoon into well-greased muffin pans and bake at 200°C for 12–15 minutes.

Golden Medley Muffins

BOWL 1: 1 cup white flour

1 cup wholemeal flour

½ cup oatmeal

2 tsp baking soda

2 tsp cinnamon

½ tsp allspice

¼ tsp cardamom

½ tsp salt

BOWL 2: 1 cup raisins

1 cup shredded apple

½ cup shredded zucchini

½ cup shredded carrot

½ cup coconut

½ cup finely chopped pecans

BOWL 3: ½ cup oil

1 cup honey

2 eggs, beaten

2 tsp vanilla essence

- Preheat oven to 180°C.

- Mix all dry ingredients in Bowl 1.

- Mix fruit, vegetables and nuts in Bowl 2.

- Mix wet ingredients in Bowl 3.

- Add contents of Bowl 3 to Bowl 1. Mix until moist.

- Fold in contents of Bowl 2.

- Three-quarters fill prepared muffin pans. Sprinkle pecans or oatmeal on top if desired.

- Bake 25–30 minutes.

Ham & Cheese Muffins

1 egg, beaten
1 cup flour
1 tblsp baking powder
1 cup grated cheese
½ cup crumbled blue cheese
1 cup chopped ham

- Make egg up to 1 cup with water and mix with remaining ingredients until just combined.

- Three-quarters fill well-greased muffin pans and bake at 200°C for 12–15 minutes.

Hazelnut Praline Muffins

½ cup chopped hazelnuts

½ cup sugar

⅓ cup oil

¾ cup sugar

1 egg

¾ cup milk

1¾ cups flour

1½ tsp baking powder

- Gently boil hazelnuts and first measure of sugar until mixture turns golden brown.

- Pour onto greased tinfoil and leave to set.

- Break praline into small pieces and crush with rolling pin or in food processor.

- Whisk oil, second measure of sugar, egg and milk together, then add dry ingredients and praline, mixing until just combined.

- Spoon into well-greased muffin pans and bake at 190°C for 20 minutes.

Hazelnut Spiced Muffins

2 cups flour

2 tsp baking powder

½ tsp salt

1 tsp ground cinnamon

⅛ tsp ground cloves

125g butter, softened

½ cup brown sugar, firmly packed

¼ cup sugar

1 egg, beaten

1 tsp grated lemon rind

½ tsp vanilla essence

1 cup milk

¾ cup ground or very finely chopped hazelnuts

¼ cup raspberry jam

sugar and cinnamon for sprinkling

- In large bowl mix together flour, baking powder, salt, cinnamon and cloves.

- In separate bowl cream butter and sugars until light and fluffy, then beat in egg, lemon rind, vanilla and milk.

- Make a well in centre of dry ingredients and add butter mixture. Stir to combine, then fold in hazelnuts.

- Spoon half the batter into prepared muffin pans.

- Put a spoonful of raspberry jam on top, then cover with remaining batter.

- Bake at 200°C for 15–20 minutes.

- Sprinkle with sugar and cinnamon mixed together.

High Protein Muffins

2½ cups bran flakes

1½ cups raisins

1¾ cups milk

1 cup wholemeal flour

1 cup soy flour

1 cup toasted wheatgerm

4 tsp baking powder

1½ tsp ground nutmeg

¾ tsp salt

4 large eggs, lightly beaten

⅔ cup honey

⅔ cup oil

¼ cup dark molasses

- Combine bran flakes, raisins and milk in large mixing bowl.

- Stir together wholemeal flour, soy flour, wheatgerm, baking powder, nutmeg and salt. Set aside.

- Combine eggs, honey, oil and molasses in small bowl and blend well.

- Add egg mixture to soaked bran flakes. Mix well.

- Add dry ingredients to bran mixture, stirring to just moisten.

- Spoon batter into prepared muffin pans, filling three-quarters full.

- Bake at 180°C for 25 minutes or until golden brown.

Honey Bran Muffins

1¼ cups wholemeal flour

1¼ cups wheat bran

2 tsp baking powder

½ tsp baking soda

1¼ cups buttermilk

¼ cup honey

1 egg

2 tblsp vegetable oil

• In large mixing bowl, combine flour, bran, baking powder and soda. Mix thoroughly.

• In small bowl, beat together buttermilk, honey, egg and oil.

• Pour wet ingredients over dry ingredients and stir until just moistened.

• Spoon batter into prepared muffin pans.

• Bake in a preheated 190°C oven for 15–20 minutes, or until lightly browned and muffins spring back to the touch. Cool slightly before serving.

Honey & Date Muffins

75g butter

½ cup honey

1½ cups chopped dates

2 eggs

¼ cup milk

1½ cups flour

2 tsp baking powder

- Heat butter and honey only long enough to melt butter. Stir in chopped dates.

- Beat eggs with milk. Sift flour and baking powder.

- Make a well in centre of flour and add honey and egg mixtures. Mix until dry ingredients are just moistened.

- Three-quarters fill greased muffin pans and bake at 200°C for 15–20 minutes or until cooked.

Hot Cross Muffins

2 cups flour

¾ cup sugar

2 tsp baking powder

½ tsp salt

¼ tsp ground cinnamon

⅛ tsp ground allspice

1 cup milk

125g butter, melted and cooled slightly

1 egg, beaten

1 tsp vanilla essence

½ tsp grated orange rind

¼ tsp grated lemon rind

1 cup currants

GLAZE

⅓ cup icing sugar

1½ tsp lemon juice

- In large bowl mix together flour, sugar, baking powder, salt, cinnamon and allspice.

- In separate bowl mix together milk, butter, egg, vanilla, orange rind and lemon rind.

- Make a well in centre of dry ingredients and add milk mixture. Stir to just combine, then fold in currants.

- Spoon batter into prepared muffin pans and bake at 190°C for 15–20 minutes.

- Drizzle a cross on the top with glaze made from icing sugar and lemon juice before serving.

Irish Coffee Muffins

2 cups flour

1 tsp baking powder

½ tsp salt

½ cup sugar

1 egg, beaten

⅓ cup butter, melted

½ cup heavy cream, unwhipped

¼ cup Irish whiskey

¼ cup coffee liqueur

• Preheat oven to 200°C.

• Sift first four ingredients together.

• Stir in remaining ingredients, until moistened.

• Three-quarters fill prepared muffin pans, and bake for approximately 20 minutes.

Jaffa Muffins

2 medium-sized oranges

125g butter, softened

1 cup sugar

2 eggs

½ cup natural yoghurt

½ cup orange juice

1 tsp baking powder

½ tsp baking soda

2 cups flour

90g dark chocolate chips

- Finely grate rind of oranges.
- In large bowl cream butter and sugar until light and fluffy. Beat in eggs and add orange rind.
- Add yoghurt, orange juice, baking powder and baking soda and stir to combine.
- Fold in flour and chocolate chips.
- Spoon batter into prepared muffin pans and bake at 190°C for 15–20 minutes.

VARIATION: If desired, top with chocolate icing and sprinkle with more chocolate chips.

Jam-Filled Muffins

1½ cups flour

¼ cup sugar

2 tsp baking powder

½ tsp baking soda

½ tsp salt

¼ cup butter

1 cup plain yoghurt

¼ cup milk

1 egg

½ tsp vanilla essence

jam

icing sugar for dusting

- Mix all dry ingredients.
- Melt butter. Take off heat and stir in yoghurt and milk. Mix.
- Beat in egg and vanilla.
- Add butter mixture to dry ingredients and stir until moistened.
- Spoon half the batter into well-greased muffin pans. Place about 1 tsp jam into each muffin and then top with remaining batter.
- Bake at 180°C for 15–20 minutes.
- Dust with icing sugar.

Kiwifruit Muffins

50g butter

¾ cup milk

2 eggs, beaten

1 cup chopped kiwifruit

2 cups flour

2 tsp baking powder

½ cup brown sugar

- Melt butter and mix with milk and eggs.

- Add to remaining ingredients and mix until just combined.

- Spoon into well-greased muffin pans and bake at 200°C for 20–25 minutes.

Kumara & Walnut Muffins

¾ cup milk

2 large eggs

¼ cup clear honey

2 tblsp oil

1 cup mashed, cooked kumara

2 cups wholemeal flour

2 tsp baking powder

½ tsp salt

1 tsp ground cinnamon

½ cup chopped walnuts

- Beat milk, eggs, honey and oil in large bowl. Stir in kumara.

- Sift flour, baking powder, salt and cinnamon and stir into kumara mixture. Add walnuts.

- Divide mixture into prepared muffin pans.

- Bake at 200°C for 20 minutes or until skewer comes out clean.

Lemon Coconut Muffins

1 cup All-bran
1½ cups skim milk
1 egg, lightly beaten
2 tblsp oil
grated rind and juice of 1 lemon
1½ cups self-raising flour
¼ cup caster sugar
½ cup coconut
extra coconut for topping

- Place All-bran and milk in large bowl and let stand for five minutes until softened.

- Stir in lightly beaten egg, oil, lemon rind and juice.

- Combine flour, sugar and coconut and stir into All-bran mixture. Mix carefully to just combine.

- Three-quarters fill greased muffin pans and sprinkle with extra coconut.

- Bake at 190°C for 25–30 minutes.

Lemon Poppy Seed Muffins

150g butter

¾ cup sugar

1 egg, beaten

rind and juice of 2 lemons

125g sour cream

1½ cups flour

1 tsp baking powder

1 tsp baking soda

3 tblsp poppy seeds

ICING

juice and rind of one lemon

icing sugar

- Cream butter and sugar, then stir in remaining ingredients until just combined.

- Spoon into muffin pans lined with paper cases and bake at 160°C for 15–20 minutes.

- When cool, top with icing made from the rind and juice of one lemon and sufficient icing sugar to make a smooth paste.

Lemon Sultana Muffins

1 cup sultanas

2 tblsp honey

rind and juice of 2 lemons

¼ cup milk

1 cup natural yoghurt

50g butter, melted

1 egg

2 cups flour

2 tsp baking powder

⅓ cup sugar

- Bring sultanas, honey and lemon rind and juice to the boil, then allow to cool.

- Add remaining ingredients and mix until just combined.

- Spoon into well-greased muffin pans and bake at 190°C for 12–15 minutes.

Lemon Tea Muffins

1 cup flour

½ cup sugar

1 tsp baking powder

1 tsp salt

½ cup fresh lemon juice

2 eggs

finely grated rind of 1 lemon

60g butter, melted and
cooled slightly

TOPPING

¼ cup melted butter

1 tblsp lemon juice

½ cup sugar

- In large bowl mix together flour, sugar, baking powder and salt.

- In separate bowl add lemon juice, eggs and lemon rind to melted butter.

- Stir into dry ingredients.

- Spoon batter into prepared muffin pans and bake at 190°C for 15–20 minutes.

- Remove from pans while still warm and brush with melted butter and lemon juice mixed together, then sprinkle with sugar.

Low-Fat Fruit Muffins

1 egg

1½ tblsp oil

¾ cup golden syrup

1¾ cups flour

2 tsp baking powder

2 tsp baking soda

¾ cup bran

1 cup unsweetened stewed apple
or other fruit

2 cups berries (blueberries,
raspberries, blackberries)

- Mix all ingredients together until just combined.

- Spoon into well-greased muffin pans and bake for 25 minutes at 200°C.

HINT: Replace stewed fruit with canned pie apple or pie fruit, such as apple and rhubarb.

Macadamia & White Chocolate Muffins

50g butter, softened

½ cup caster sugar

1 egg

1 cup milk

2 cups flour

2 tsp baking powder

160g white chocolate, chopped

1 cup chopped macadamia nuts

- Cream butter and sugar until fluffy.

- Stir in eggs and milk.

- Mix in flour, baking powder, chocolate and nuts until just combined.

- Three-quarters fill well-greased muffin pans and bake at 190°C for 20 minutes.

Maggie's Garden Muffins

1½ cups flour

1 cup wholemeal flour

4 tsp baking powder

½ tsp salt

1 large egg

2 large egg whites

⅔ cup skim milk

⅓ cup virgin olive oil

1 cup grated zucchini

3 tblsp minced fresh basil

1 tsp minced garlic

⅓ cup freshly grated Romano cheese

½ cup pine nuts

- Sift flours, baking powder and salt into large bowl.

- In small bowl, whisk together egg, egg whites, milk and oil until well blended.

- Add egg mixture to dry ingredients and mix gently.

- Stir in zucchini, basil, garlic, cheese and pine nuts and mix until just combined.

- Three-quarters fill greased muffin pans and bake at 220°C for about 20 minutes.

Maple Nut Muffins

1 cup wholemeal flour

1 cup flour

2½ tsp baking powder

¼ tsp baking soda

½ tsp salt

½ cup sugar

½ cup chopped nuts

1 egg

½ cup milk

¼ cup maple syrup

¼ cup oil

½ cup sour cream

- In large bowl mix together flours, baking powder, baking soda, salt, sugar and nuts.

- In separate bowl mix together egg, milk, maple syrup, oil and sour cream.

- Add milk mixture to dry ingredients and stir until just moistened.

- Spoon batter into prepared muffin pans and bake at 200°C for 20 minutes.

Marbled Muffins

¼ cup milk

1 egg

50g butter, melted

1 cup natural yoghurt

1 tsp vanilla essence

2 cups flour

2 tsp baking powder

⅓ cup sugar

1 tsp red food colouring

2 tblsp cocoa mixed with
2 tblsp milk

50g chocolate, grated (optional)

- Mix milk, egg, butter, yoghurt and vanilla together.

- Add flour, baking powder and sugar and mix until just combined.

- Put 1 tablespoon of mixture into well-greased muffin pans.

- Divide remaining mixture between two bowls. To one bowl add food colouring, to the other add cocoa mixture and grated chocolate.

- Put spoonfuls of each mixture into muffin pans and give a quick swirl with a knife.

- Bake at 190°C for 15–20 minutes.

Mexican Muffins

2 eggs, beaten

¾ cup water

1 cup refried beans

1 cup flour

1 tsp salt

1 tblsp baking powder

1 cup grated cheese

2 spring onions, chopped

3 tomatoes, chopped

grated cheese for sprinkling

- Mix all ingredients together until just combined.

- Spoon into well-greased muffin pans and sprinkle with extra grated cheese.

- Bake at 200°C for 15–20 minutes.

Muesli Muffins

1½ cups self-raising flour

100g butter

1½ cups muesli

1 apple, peeled, cored and grated

½ cup brown sugar

¼ cup chopped nuts (optional)

½ cup milk

½ cup water

- Sift flour and rub in butter until mixture resembles breadcrumbs.

- Add remaining ingredients and mix until just combined.

- Three-quarters fill well-greased muffin pans and bake at 190°C for 20–25 minutes.

Oat & Orange Muffins

1 orange, peeled and quartered

2 cups oat bran

¼ cup raw sugar

1 tsp mixed spice

2 tsp baking powder

¾ cup sultanas

¼ cup wheatgerm

2 tblsp oil

¾ cup milk

1 tsp baking soda

¼ cup chopped walnuts
for topping

- Remove pips and place orange in food processor. Process until finely chopped.

- In mixing bowl, combine oat bran, sugar, mixed spice, baking powder, sultanas and wheatgerm.

- Heat oil and milk slightly and dissolve baking soda in milk mixture.

- Add oat bran mixture and milk to orange in the food processor. Pulse to just combine.

- Three-quarters fill greased muffin pans, sprinkle with walnuts and bake at 190°C for 15 minutes or until firm.

Oaty Apple Walnut Muffins

100g butter

2 tsp grated lemon rind

¾ cup brown sugar

1 egg

1 cup self-raising flour

½ tsp cinnamon

¼ tsp baking soda

¼ tsp salt

¾ cup unsweetened stewed apple

1 cup quick-cooking rolled oats

½ cup sultanas

½ cup chopped walnuts

- Cream butter, lemon rind and sugar. Add egg and beat well.

- Sift flour, cinnamon, baking soda and salt, and add alternately to creamed mixture with stewed apples.

- Fold in oats, sultanas and walnuts.

- Three-quarters fill greased muffin pans and bake at 180°C for 20–25 minutes.

Olive Muffins

1 cup (300g) chopped pitted black olives

2 cups flour

½ cup grated onion

¾ cup olive oil, plus additional oil to brush muffin pans

1½ tblsp chopped fresh mint, or 1 tsp crushed dried mint

1 tblsp sugar

1 heaped tsp baking powder

- Preheat oven to 190°C.
- Rinse olives and drain. Dry on paper towels.
- Combine all ingredients, adding baking powder last.
- Brush muffin pans with oil and dust with flour.
- Bake for 20–25 minutes, or until golden.

Olive & Chilli Muffins

1 egg
¾ cup water
2 cups flour
½ tsp salt
1 tblsp baking powder
1½ cups grated cheddar
½ cup pitted black olives, sliced
1 tsp whole dried chilli,
very finely sliced
2 tblsp cornmeal

- Mix all ingredients except cornmeal until just combined.
- Spoon into well-greased muffin pans and sprinkle with cornmeal.
- Bake at 200°C for 12–15 minutes.

Olive & Salami Muffins

1 egg, beaten
1 cup flour
¼ tsp salt
1 tblsp baking powder
½ cup grated cheese
⅔ cup pitted black olives, sliced
⅔ cup cubed spicy salami

- Make egg up to one cup with water and mix with remaining ingredients until just combined.

- Three-quarters fill well-greased muffin pans and bake at 200°C for 12–15 minutes.

Orange Muffins

rind and flesh of 2 oranges
(pith and seeds discarded)

75g butter, softened

1 egg

1½ cups self-raising flour

¾ cup sugar

½ cup currants

- Process orange rind and flesh with butter and egg.

- Mix in remaining ingredients until just combined.

- Spoon into well-greased muffin pans and bake at 190°C for 15–20 minutes.

Orange Carrot Muffins

1½ cups wholemeal flour

½ cup oat bran

2 tsp baking powder

½ tsp baking soda

1 tsp cinnamon

1 egg

⅔ cup orange juice

½ cup buttermilk

2 tblsp sugar

1 tsp grated orange peel

2 tblsp oil

1 cup coarsely grated carrot

- In large bowl, mix together flour, oat bran, baking powder, baking soda and cinnamon.

- In separate bowl, beat together egg, juice, buttermilk, sugar, orange peel and oil. Mixture will look curdled, but don't worry.

- Stir in carrot.

- Add wet ingredients to dry ingredients, and stir until just moistened.

- Divide batter between muffin pans.

- Bake for approximately 20 minutes in a 200°C oven.

Orange Chocolate Chip Muffins

2 cups flour

½ cup brown sugar, firmly packed

½ cup sugar

1½ tsp baking powder

½ tsp baking soda

½ tsp salt

⅓ cup oil

¼ cup orange juice

¼ cup orange liqueur

1 egg

1 tsp grated orange rind

1 tsp vanilla essence

1 cup chocolate chips

icing sugar or cocoa for dusting

- In large bowl mix together flour, sugars, baking powder, baking soda and salt.

- In separate bowl mix together oil, orange juice, liqueur, egg, orange rind and vanilla.

- Make well in centre of dry ingredients and add orange mixture.

- Stir to combine, then fold in chocolate chips.

- Spoon batter into prepared muffin pans and bake at 200°C for 15–20 minutes.

- Serve dusted with icing sugar or cocoa.

VARIATION: Top with orange icing and sprinkle with chocolate chips.

Orange Toasted Almond Muffins

2½ cups flour

1 cup sugar

3½ tsp baking powder

½ tsp salt

¼ tsp almond essence

1 tblsp grated orange rind

⅓ cup oil

¾ cup evaporated milk

½ cup water

1 egg

1 cup toasted finely chopped
almonds

ICING

1 cup sifted icing sugar

1–2 tblsp orange juice

2 tsp orange rind

- In large bowl combine flour, sugar, baking powder, salt, almond essence, orange rind, oil, evaporated milk, water and egg. Beat with electric mixer at high speed for 30 seconds until blended.

- Fold in ¾ cup chopped almonds.

- Spoon batter into prepared muffin pans to two-thirds full.

- Bake at 190°C for 15–18 minutes.

- In small bowl combine icing sugar, orange juice and rind. Spread over muffins. Sprinkle with remaining almonds.

Overnight Bran Muffins

1 egg
1½ cups natural yoghurt
½ cup oil
1½ cups flour
1 tsp baking soda
1 tsp ground cinnamon
1½ cups bran
½ cup brown sugar
125g dates, chopped

- Mix all ingredients together until just combined.

- Cover mixture and leave in fridge for up to 24 hours.

- Spoon into well-greased muffin pans and bake at 180°C for 15–20 minutes.

Passionfruit Crunch Muffins

1 egg
½ cup milk
⅓ cup honey
⅓ cup oil
2 cups flour
1 tsp baking powder
½ cup passionfruit pulp

TOPPING
50g butter
½ cup brown sugar
½ cup rolled oats

- Mix all muffin ingredients together until just combined.

- Three-quarters fill well-greased muffin pans and sprinkle with topping made by rubbing butter and sugar together and mixing in rolled oats.

- Bake at 180°C for 15–20 minutes.

Passover Ginger Muffins

¾ cup potato flour or rice flour

½ tsp ground cinnamon

½ tsp ground ginger

⅛ tsp ground cloves

1 whole egg

2 tblsp honey

2 tsp freshly grated orange peel

2 tblsp freshly squeezed orange juice

4 egg whites

2 tblsp sugar

- In large bowl, mix together potato flour and spices.

- In small bowl, whisk together whole egg, honey, orange peel and juice. Add to dry ingredients, and stir together until just blended. Batter will be stiff.

- In deep, medium-sized bowl, beat egg whites until soft peaks form. Add sugar, and beat until whites are thick and glossy.

- Stir about a quarter of egg white mixture into potato flour batter, then fold in remaining egg whites.

- Spoon batter into muffin pans and bake at 200°C for about 15 minutes.

- Let cool for about 10 minutes before removing from pans. Best served warm.

Peach Muffins

2 cups canned or fresh peaches, drained

4 cups flour

2 cups sugar

2 tsp baking powder

½ tsp salt

3 eggs

¾ cup oil

2 cups milk

TOPPING

½ cup sugar

1 tsp cinnamon

- Dice drained peaches to the size of peas.

- Mix flour, sugar, baking powder and salt. Set aside.

- In separate bowl combine eggs, oil and milk.

- Add flour mixture and combine gently. Fold in peaches.

- Spoon into prepared muffin pans, sprinkle with topping and bake in preheated oven at 200°C for 20–25 minutes.

Peanut Butter Muffins

1½ cups flour

2 tsp baking powder

½ cup sugar

½ tsp salt

60g butter

½ cup crunchy peanut butter

2 eggs, beaten

1 cup milk

- In large bowl mix together flour, baking powder, sugar and salt.

- Cut in butter and peanut butter and mix until crumbly.

- Add eggs and milk and stir until just combined.

- Spoon batter into prepared muffin pans and bake at 190°C for 15–20 minutes.

VARIATION: Brush tops of hot muffins with melted jam, then sprinkle with chopped peanuts.

Pear & Honey Muffins

1 egg

1 cup natural yoghurt

¼ cup lemon juice

50g butter, melted

½ cup honey

2 cups wholemeal flour

1 tsp baking powder

1 tsp baking soda

½ cup brown sugar

2 large pears, peeled,
cored and diced

honey for pouring

- Mix all ingredients together until just combined.

- Three-quarters fill well-greased muffin pans and bake at 190°C for 15–20 minutes.

- Pour a little extra honey on top of each muffin while still warm.

Pecan Cinnamon Muffins

1½ cups flour, sifted

¼ cup sugar

¼ cup brown sugar, packed

2 tsp baking powder

½ tsp salt

½ tsp ground cinnamon

1 large egg, lightly beaten

½ cup oil

½ cup milk

½ cup chopped pecans

- Sift flour, sugar, brown sugar, baking powder, salt and cinnamon into mixing bowl.

- Combine egg, oil and milk in small bowl and blend well.

- Add to dry ingredients, stirring just enough to moisten. Fold in pecans.

- Spoon batter into greased muffin pans, filling each two-thirds full.

- Bake in 200°C oven for 20 minutes or until golden brown.

Persimmon Muffins

1 cup wholemeal flour

1 cup flour

1 tsp baking powder

½ tsp salt

½ tsp ground cinnamon

½ tsp ground nutmeg

¼ tsp ground cloves

½ cup mashed persimmon pulp

½ cup raisins

1 egg

½ cup milk

⅓ cup oil

½ cup honey

ICING

1½ cups icing sugar

½ tsp vanilla essence

2 tblsp brandy

- Mix together flours, baking powder, salt and spices.

- In separate bowl mix together remaining ingredients.

- Add liquid ingredients to dry ingredients and combine until just moistened.

- Spoon batter into prepared muffin pans and bake at 200°C for 18 minutes.

- Allow to cool before icing.

- To make icing, mix ingredients together thoroughly.

Pineapple Muffins

2 cups flour

1 tsp baking powder

1 cup sugar

1 tsp salt

1 egg

1 cup milk

1 tblsp butter, melted

½ cup drained, crushed pineapple

- Sift dry ingredients.

- Beat egg with milk, and add butter and pineapple.

- Make a well in centre of dry ingredients, add liquid and stir until just damp and lumpy.

- Three-quarters fill greased muffin pans and bake at 200°C for 15–20 minutes.

Pine Nut & Yoghurt Muffins

2 cups flour

¼ cup sugar

1 tsp baking soda

¼ tsp salt

1 cup natural yoghurt

¼ cup milk

60g butter, melted and
cooled slightly

1 egg

2 tblsp honey

1 tsp vanilla essence

¾ cup chopped dried apricots

½ cup chopped pine nuts

- In large bowl stir together flour, sugar, baking soda and salt.

- In separate bowl mix together yoghurt, milk, butter, egg, honey and vanilla until well combined.

- Make a well in centre of dry ingredients and add yoghurt mixture. Stir to just combine.

- Mix in apricots and all but 2 tablespoons of pine nuts.

- Spoon batter into prepared muffin pans and sprinkle with reserved pine nuts.

- Bake at 200°C for 15–20 minutes.

Pistachio Muffins

1 egg

½ cup water

50g butter, melted

1 cup natural yoghurt

2 cups flour

¼ tsp salt

2 tsp baking powder

¼ cup sugar

1 cup chopped pistachio nuts

- Mix all ingredients together until just combined.

- Spoon into well-greased muffin pans and bake at 190°C for 15–20 minutes.

Pistachio Chocolate Muffins

⅓ cup butter

2 cups flour

3 tsp baking powder

1 tsp salt

⅓ cup sugar

2 eggs

1 cup milk

2 tsp rum

½ cup chopped pistachio nuts

½ cup chocolate bits

⅓ cup finely chopped pistachio nuts

- Rub butter into flour, baking powder and salt. Add sugar.

- Beat eggs, milk and rum.

- Make a well in centre of dry ingredients and add milk mixture, chopped nuts and chocolate bits. Mix very lightly until just combined.

- Three-quarters fill greased muffin pans and sprinkle with finely chopped pistachio nuts.

- Bake at 200°C for 20–25 minutes.

Pizza Muffins

2 cups flour

½ tsp salt

1 tblsp baking powder

1 onion, chopped

1 cup grated cheese

1 rasher bacon, cooked and chopped

1 tomato, chopped

1 egg, lightly beaten

- Mix first seven ingredients together.

- Make egg up to 1 cup with water, then mix with dry ingredients until just combined.

- Spoon into well-greased muffin pans and bake at 200°C for 20 minutes.

Plum Muffins

10 to 12 dark ripe plums
3 cups flour
1 tblsp baking powder
¾ cup sugar
1 tblsp grated lemon rind
50g butter, melted
2 eggs, lightly beaten
1¼ cups milk
extra 2 tblsp sugar

- Peel and stone plums, and roughly chop flesh. Set aside.

- Sift flour and baking powder and stir in first measure of sugar and lemon rind.

- Combine melted butter and lightly beaten eggs, and add milk.

- Pour milk mixture into flour. Gently stir to just mix. Fold in chopped plums.

- Three-quarters fill greased muffin pans. Sprinkle with extra sugar.

- Bake at 200°C for 15–20 minutes.

Potato Fry Muffins

2 potatoes, peeled and cubed

1 clove garlic, crushed

1 tsp mustard seeds

1 tsp turmeric

1 tblsp oil

1 egg, lightly beaten

1 cup flour

1 tblsp baking powder

1 tsp salt

1 cup grated cheese

- Fry potato with garlic, mustard seeds, turmeric and oil until potato is tender but not soft. Beware – the mustard seeds may jump around.

- Transfer to a bowl.

- Make egg up to 1 cup with water.

- Add egg and remaining ingredients to potato mixture and stir until just combined.

- Spoon into well-greased muffin pans and bake at 180°C for 12–15 minutes.

Potato & Sun-Dried Tomato Muffins

3 cups peeled and grated potatoes

1 clove garlic, finely chopped

8 sun-dried tomatoes, finely chopped

½ cup flour

½ tsp salt

1 tsp baking powder

3 tblsp olive oil

2 egg yolks

2 egg whites, beaten to a soft snow

• Rinse and drain potatoes.

• Mix with all ingredients except egg whites.

• Fold in egg whites.

• Spoon into greased muffin pans.

• Bake at 200°C for 20–25 minutes.

Pumpkin Muffins

2 tblsp butter
½ cup sugar
1 egg
¾ cup flour
1 tsp baking powder
1 tsp baking soda
½ tsp ground cinnamon
¼ tsp ground nutmeg
¾ cup wholemeal flour
¼ cup sultanas
½ cup mashed cooked pumpkin
milk to mix

• Cream butter and sugar, then add egg and beat.

• Sift flour, baking powder, baking soda and spices into creamed mixture.

• Stir in wholemeal flour, sultanas, pumpkin and sufficient milk to make a moist mixture.

• Spoon batter into prepared muffin pans and bake at 180°C for 15–20 minutes.

• If desired, ice with cream cheese and icing sugar mixed together.

Pumpkin & Chocolate Chip Muffins

1 cup sliced almonds

1¾ cups flour

1 tsp allspice

1 tsp garam masala

¼ tsp baking powder

1 tsp baking soda

¼ tsp salt

1 cup sugar

2 eggs

1 cup cooked mashed pumpkin

150g butter, melted

1 cup chocolate chips

- Place almonds on oven tray and bake at 180°C for about five minutes or until lightly browned.

- Sift flour, allspice, garam masala, baking powder, baking soda and salt. Add sugar.

- In separate bowl, beat eggs and add pumpkin and melted butter. Beat to combine.

- Fold almonds and chocolate chips into this mixture.

- Quickly fold in dry ingredients.

- Three-quarters fill greased muffin pans and bake at 180°C for 20 minutes or until well risen.

Raisin Muffins

1½ cups wholemeal flour

⅓ cup brown sugar

3 tsp baking powder

½ tsp salt

1 tsp cinnamon

½ cup wheatgerm

¾ cup raisins

⅔ cup milk

⅓ cup oil

2 eggs, lightly beaten

- Sift flour, adding any husks in sifter to the bowl.

- Mix in sugar, baking powder, salt, cinnamon, wheatgerm and raisins.

- Add milk, oil and lightly beaten eggs. Mix until dry ingredients are just moistened.

- Three-quarters fill greased muffin pans and bake at 200°C for 20 minutes.

Rhubarb Muffins

2 cups flour

4 tsp baking powder

½ tsp salt

¾ cup sugar

1 cup milk

100g butter, melted and cooled slightly

1 egg

1½ cups finely chopped rhubarb

3 tblsp raw sugar for sprinkling

1 tblsp ground cinnamon for sprinkling

- Sift together flour, baking powder and salt. Add sugar and combine.

- In separate bowl mix together milk, butter and egg.

- Add milk mixture to dry ingredients and combine, then stir in rhubarb.

- Spoon batter into prepared muffin pans.

- Mix together raw sugar and cinnamon and sprinkle over.

- Bake at 220°C for 15 minutes.

- Delicious served with whipped cream.

Rocky Road Muffins

¼ cup milk

1 egg

1 cup natural yoghurt

50g butter, melted

2 cups flour

1 tsp baking powder

½ cup sugar

½ cup small marshmallows

½ cup roughly chopped chocolate

½ cup peanuts

½ cup jubes

- Mix milk, egg, yoghurt and butter.
- Add remaining ingredients and mix until just combined.
- Spoon into well-greased muffin pans and bake at 180°C for 12–15 minutes.

HINT: Top with icing made from 1 tablespoon each cocoa, butter and milk heated together and mixed with sufficient icing sugar to make a paste. Place marshmallows or jubes in icing before it sets.

Salmon Muffins

1 × 185g can salmon, drained and
mashed (reserve liquid)

1 egg

1 cup flour

1 tsp salt

1 tblsp baking powder

1 cup grated mild cheese

- Make liquid from salmon up to ¾ cup with water and mix into remaining ingredients until just combined.

- Three-quarters fill well-greased muffin pans and bake at 200°C for 12–15 minutes.

HINT: Make a small diagonal split in the top of each muffin before serving, spread with cream cheese and tuck in a small piece of smoked salmon.

Self-Saucing Chocolate Muffins

½ cup white sugar

1 cup self-raising flour

1 tblsp cocoa

½ cup milk

1 tblsp butter, melted

1 tblsp cocoa

1 cup brown sugar

1½ cups boiling water

- Mix white sugar, flour and first measure of cocoa in a bowl.

- Add milk and melted butter, stir until just combined and half fill well-greased muffin pans with mixture.

- Mix second measure of cocoa with brown sugar and boiling water, and add to each muffin pan to take level up to three-quarters full.

- Bake at 180°C for 15–20 minutes.

- To turn muffins out, place serving dish over muffin pans and carefully flip over. Scoop out any remaining sauce.

Sliced Banana Muffins

1½ cups flour

⅓ cup sugar

50g butter

1 tsp baking powder

2 bananas, thinly sliced

1 egg

½ cup milk

100g chocolate, chopped

- Rub flour, sugar and butter together until mixture resembles breadcrumbs.

- Add remaining ingredients and mix until just combined.

- Spoon into well-greased muffin pans and bake at 190°C for 20 minutes.

Sour Cream Jalapeno Corn Muffins

1½ cups yellow cornmeal

½ cup flour

1 tblsp granulated sugar

1 tblsp baking powder

1 tsp salt

2 large eggs

1 cup sour cream

1–1½ tsp minced and seeded jalapeno pepper

- Thoroughly mix cornmeal, flour, sugar, baking powder and salt in large bowl.

- Beat eggs and sour cream with a whisk or fork in a small bowl. When smooth, stir in jalapeno pepper.

- Pour over flour mixture. Fold in with a rubber spatula until well mixed. Batter will be very stiff.

- Scoop batter into well-greased muffin pans.

- Bake at 180°C for 20–25 minutes, or until firm to the touch in the centre.

- Let cool 5 minutes in pans before turning out onto a cooling rack.

Spiced Apple Muffins

2 eggs

1 cup water

2 cups wholemeal flour

¼ tsp salt

1 tblsp baking powder

1 tsp ground cinnamon

1 tsp mixed spice

½ cup brown sugar

2 cups cooked apple cubes
(or canned pie apple)

coffee sugar

- Mix together all ingredients except coffee sugar until just combined.

- Three-quarters fill well-greased muffin pans and sprinkle with coffee sugar.

- Bake at 190°C for 20–25 minutes.

Spiced Lemon Muffins

2 cups flour

1½ tsp ground cinnamon

4 tsp baking powder

1 tblsp grated lemon rind

½ cup sugar

2 eggs

½ cup oil

1 cup natural yoghurt

¼ cup milk

¼ cup raw sugar for sprinkling

1 tsp ground cinnamon
for sprinkling

TOPPING

2 eggs

½ cup sugar

grated rind & juice of 2 lemons

2 tblsp butter

- In large bowl mix flour, cinnamon, baking powder, lemon rind and sugar.

- In separate bowl beat eggs, oil, yoghurt and milk.

- Add yoghurt mixture to dry ingredients, stir to combine.

- Spoon into prepared muffin pans and sprinkle with raw sugar and cinnamon mixed together.

- Bake at 200°C for 15–20 minutes.

- To make topping, combine eggs and sugar in heatproof bowl. Stir in lemon rind, lemon juice and butter. Cook in bowl over saucepan of boiling water for 15 minutes, stirring occasionally, until mixture thickens. Spread on cooled muffins.

Spicy All-Bran Muffins

1¼ cups All-bran
1½ cups skim milk
1 egg yolk
60g butter, melted
½ cup chopped raisins or dates
1½ cups self-raising flour
1 tsp cinnamon
½ tsp nutmeg
¼ cup caster sugar
2 egg whites, stiffly beaten
extra All-bran for topping

- Place All-bran and milk in large bowl and let stand for five minutes until softened.

- Beat in egg yolk, melted butter and raisins.

- Sift flour and spices. Stir in sugar and add to All-bran mixture.

- Fold in stiffly beaten egg whites.

- Three-quarters fill greased muffin pans and sprinkle with extra All-bran.

- Bake at 200°C for 25–30 minutes.

Spicy Fruit Muffins

50g butter

½ cup sugar

1 egg

1 grated apple

½ tsp baking soda

1 dessertspoon boiling water

¾ cup flour

½ tsp cinnamon

½ tsp mixed spice

¼ cup sultanas

- Cream butter and sugar.
- Add egg and beat well.
- Stir in grated apple, soda dissolved in water, flour and spices. Mix lightly, then fold in sultanas.
- Three-quarters fill greased muffin pans and bake at 200°C for 15 minutes or until firm.

Spicy Nut Muffins

1 tblsp olive oil

1 cup nuts (almonds, peanuts, cashews, walnuts)

1 garlic clove, crushed

1 tsp salt

¼ tsp each ground cumin, coriander, chilli powder, ginger and cinnamon

1 egg, beaten

¼ cup water

1 cup natural yoghurt

50g butter, melted

2 tblsp honey

2 cups self-raising flour

- Heat oil in frying pan and gently fry nuts, garlic, salt and spices for 15 minutes. Leave to cool.

- Mix remaining ingredients together until just combined.

- Add nuts, reserving ¼ cup for decoration.

- Three-quarters fill well-greased muffin pans and sprinkle with reserved nuts.

- Bake at 200°C for 15–20 minutes.

Spicy Prune Muffins

1 tsp baking soda

¾ cup warm milk

1 egg

⅓ cup oil

2 cups self-raising flour

1 tsp mixed spice

½ cup brown sugar

¾ cup prunes soaked in
¼ cup liqueur

- Stir baking soda into milk.

- Mix remaining ingredients until just combined, then add milk mixture and stir gently to mix.

- Spoon into well-greased muffin pans and bake at 190°C for 20–25 minutes.

Spicy Pumpkin Muffins

1 cup plain flour

1 cup wholemeal flour

¼ cup sugar

1 tblsp baking powder

½ tblsp each ground cinnamon and nutmeg

½ tsp each ground ginger and cloves

2 eggs

¼ cup oil

¾ cup low-fat milk

1 cup pumpkin purée

- In large bowl, mix dry ingredients.
- In separate bowl, beat together eggs, oil, milk and pumpkin.
- Add to dry ingredients and stir until just combined.
- Spoon into prepared muffin pans.
- Bake at 200°C for 20–25 minutes.

Spinach & Caramelised Onion Muffins

2 onions, diced

1 tsp olive oil

1 bunch spinach, washed and spun dry

2½ cups flour

¼ cup sugar

1 tsp baking powder

2 tsp salt

2 eggs

¾ cup milk

⅔ cup oil

½ cup grated Parmesan cheese for topping

- Cook the diced onions slowly over medium-high heat in olive oil until they become richly caramelised. Remove to cool.

- Add the spinach to the pan and cook over high heat until the leaves become completely wilted. Remove to cool. When cool, chop finely. Reserve.

- Combine four dry ingredients in bowl and mix.

- Add eggs, milk and oil to dry ingredients along with cooled onions and spinach. Mix together until just combined.

- Scoop batter into buttered muffin pans, filling two-thirds full. Sprinkle tops of batter with Parmesan cheese.

- Bake at 215°C for about 15 minutes.

Spinach & Feta Muffins

1 egg

¾ cup water

2 cups self-raising flour

½ tsp salt

1 clove garlic, crushed

100g feta cheese, crumbled

1 cup finely shredded spinach

⅔ cup grated cheddar

¼ cup grated Parmesan cheese

- Mix together all ingredients except Parmesan cheese until just combined.

- Spoon into well-greased muffin pans and sprinkle with Parmesan.

- Bake at 180°C for 15–20 minutes.

Strawberry Muffins

3 cups flour

½ cup sugar

½ cup brown sugar

1 tblsp baking powder

125g butter, melted and cooled slightly

3 eggs

1 cup milk

1½ cups chopped strawberries

icing sugar for dusting

- In large bowl mix together flour, sugars and baking powder.

- In separate bowl mix together butter, eggs and milk.

- Add to dry ingredients then fold in berries.

- Brush oil onto bottoms of muffin pans only. Spoon batter into pans and bake at 200°C for 20 minutes.

- Serve hot, dusted with icing sugar.

VARIATION: Allow muffins to cool and serve with fresh whipped cream and strawberries.

Strawberry Rhubarb Muffins

1 cup rolled oats
1 cup strawberry yoghurt
125g butter, melted
½ cup brown sugar
1 egg
1 cup flour
½ tsp salt
1 tsp baking powder
½ tsp baking soda
1 tsp cinnamon
¾ cup bran
¾ cup finely chopped rhubarb
6 tblsp strawberry jam

- Soak rolled oats in strawberry yoghurt for five minutes.

- Stir melted butter and brown sugar into yoghurt.

- Lightly beat egg and add to yoghurt mixture.

- Sift flour, salt, baking powder, baking soda and cinnamon and add with bran to yoghurt mixture. Stir until dry ingredients are just moistened.

- Fold in chopped rhubarb and strawberry jam.

- Three-quarters fill greased muffin pans and bake at 190°C for 15–20 minutes.

Strawberry Yoghurt Muffins

1¾ cups wholemeal flour

½ cup caster sugar

2 eggs, beaten

60g butter, melted and cooled slightly

⅔ cup milk

⅓ cup strawberry yoghurt

coconut for sprinkling

- In large bowl mix together flour and sugar.

- In separate bowl mix together eggs, butter and milk.

- Add milk mixture to dry ingredients and stir until just combined.

- Spoon batter into prepared muffin pans and bake at 190°C for 15–20 minutes.

- Allow to cool, then slice off tops and cut each top in half. Drop a teaspoonful of yoghurt onto cut surface of muffin and push straight edges of tops into yoghurt. Sprinkle with coconut.

Sultana Bran Muffins

1⅓ cups flour

1½ tblsp baking powder

¼ tsp salt

½ tsp cinnamon

1⅓ cups milk

3 cups sultana bran

2 eggs, well beaten

¼ cup melted butter

½ cup honey

- Sift together flour, baking powder, salt and cinnamon.

- Pour milk over sultana bran, stir, and let stand 5 minutes.

- Stir in eggs, melted butter and honey.

- Add dry ingredients and stir just until moistened.

- Spoon batter into greased muffin pans.

- Bake at 200°C for 20 minutes.

Sultana & Pineapple Muffins

1 × 450g can crushed pineapple

1 cup sultanas

1 cup sugar

125g butter

1 tsp mixed spice

¼ tsp salt

2 eggs

2 cups flour

1½ tsp baking powder

icing sugar for dusting

- Tip crushed pineapple into a saucepan and add sultanas, sugar, butter, mixed spice and salt. Bring to the boil, stirring, until butter melts. Simmer for 5 minutes, then allow to cool slightly.

- Beat in eggs.

- Combine flour and baking powder and add to pineapple mixture. Stir to combine.

- Spoon batter into prepared muffin pans and bake at 180°C for 15–20 minutes.

- Serve dusted with icing sugar.

VARIATION: If desired, fill with whipped cream mixed with drained crushed pineapple.

Sultana Sesame Muffins

2 cups flour

¼ cup sugar

4 tsp baking powder

1 tsp salt (optional)

½ tsp ginger

¼ tsp cinnamon

¾ cup chopped sultanas

1 egg

1 cup milk

⅓ cup butter, melted

TOPPING

1 tblsp sesame seeds

1 tblsp brown sugar

pinch of ginger

- Sift flour, sugar, baking powder, salt, first measure of ginger and cinnamon. Add sultanas and mix well.

- In small bowl, beat egg and add milk and melted butter.

- Stir into flour mixture until just combined.

- Three-quarters fill greased muffin pans.

- Combine sesame seeds, brown sugar and pinch of ginger and sprinkle over muffins.

- Bake at 220°C for 20–25 minutes.

Sun-Dried Tomato
& Herb Muffins

1 egg, beaten

1 cup flour

¼ tsp salt

1 tblsp baking powder

2 tblsp chopped fresh herbs

1½ cups grated cheese

½ cup sun-dried tomatoes
in oil, chopped

- Make egg up to one cup with water and mix with remaining ingredients until just combined.

- Three-quarters fill well-greased muffin pans and bake at 200°C for 12–15 minutes.

Sweet Sherry Currant Muffins

½ cup currants

2 tblsp sweet sherry

100g butter, softened

½ cup packed brown sugar

2 eggs

2 cups plain flour

3 tsp baking powder

½ tsp baking soda

½ tsp salt

1¼ cups buttermilk
(or soured milk)

TOPPING

2 tblsp caster sugar

1 tsp cinnamon

- Soak currants in sherry until plump.

- Beat softened butter and brown sugar until fluffy.

- Beat in eggs then stir in currants.

- Sift flour, baking powder, baking soda and salt, and fold into creamed mixture alternately with buttermilk. Mix until just combined.

- Three-quarters fill greased muffin pans.

- Combine caster sugar and cinnamon and sprinkle over muffins.

- Bake at 200°C for 15 minutes until browned.

Tamarillo & Spice Muffins

2 cups flour

½ cup sugar

2½ tsp baking powder

2 tsp mixed spice

1 egg, beaten

½ cup milk

100g butter, melted and
cooled slightly

4 tamarillos, peeled and chopped

FILLING

whipped cream

sugar

chopped tamarillo

- In large bowl mix together flour, sugar, baking powder and mixed spice.

- In separate bowl mix together egg, milk and butter.

- Add milk mixture and tamarillos to dry ingredients and stir to just combine.

- Spoon batter into prepared muffin pans and bake at 200°C for 20 minutes.

- Serve filled with sweetened whipped cream into which chopped tamarillo has been folded.

Tapenade & Olive Muffins

1 egg, beaten
½ cup tapenade
½ cup grated cheese
1 cup whole green olives
1 cup flour
1 tblsp baking powder
¼ tsp salt

- Make egg up to one cup with water. Add tapenade, then stir in remaining ingredients until just combined.

- Three-quarters fill well-greased muffin pans and bake at 200°C for 12–15 minutes.

Three-Grain Pear Muffins

2 pears

1 large egg, beaten

1 cup buttermilk

2 tblsp oil

1¼ cups wholemeal flour

¾ cup cornmeal

½ cup rolled oats

¼ cup chopped raisins or currants

1½ tsp baking powder

½ tsp baking soda

1 tsp cinnamon

- Quarter and core the pears, but do not peel. Grate the pears.

- Beat together egg, buttermilk and oil. Add pears.

- In separate bowl, combine remaining ingredients.

- Add wet ingredients to dry ingredients, and stir until just blended.

- Spoon into prepared muffin pans.

- Bake in a preheated 180°C oven for about 20–25 minutes.

Toasted Pine Nut Muffins

1 egg

¼ cup water

1 cup natural yoghurt

50g butter, melted

2 tblsp honey

2 cups flour

1 tblsp baking powder

90g ground almonds

⅓ cup sugar

¾ cup pine nuts, pan-fried
until light brown

honey for pouring

- Mix all ingredients together until just combined.

- Spoon into well-greased muffin pans and bake at 190°C for 15–20 minutes.

- Pour a little warmed honey over each muffin while still hot.

Toffee Muffins

½ cup sugar
½ cup water
⅓ cup oil
¾ cup sugar
1 egg
¾ cup milk
1¾ cups flour
1½ tsp baking powder

- Gently boil first measure of sugar with water until mixture turns golden brown.

- Pour onto greased aluminium foil and leave to set.

- Break toffee into small pieces.

- Reserve some larger pieces for decorating cooked muffins.

- Whisk oil, second measure of sugar, egg and milk together.

- Add toffee and remaining ingredients, and mix until just combined.

- Spoon into well-greased muffin pans and bake at 190°C for 20 minutes.

Toffee Walnut Muffins

½ cup sugar
½ cup water
⅓ cup oil
¾ cup sugar
1 egg
¾ cup milk
2¼ cups flour
1½ tsp baking powder
1 cup walnut pieces
12 walnut halves for decoration

- Boil first measure of sugar and water gently until mixture turns golden brown.

- Pour onto greased aluminium foil. When set, break toffee into small pieces.

- Whisk oil, second measure of sugar, egg and milk together. Add toffee and remaining ingredients, mixing until just combined.

- Three-quarters fill well-greased muffin pans and put a walnut half on top of each.

- Bake at 190°C for 20 minutes.

Tomato, Cheese & Oregano Muffins

1 egg

¾ cup water

1½ cups self-raising flour

1 cup grated tasty cheddar cheese

¼ cup grated Parmesan cheese

1 tblsp fresh oregano
(or 1 tsp dried)

3 tomatoes, seeded and chopped

- Mix all ingredients together until just combined.

- Spoon into well-greased muffin pans and bake at 190°C for 15 minutes.

Upside-Down Rhubarb Muffins

¼ cup melted butter

1 cup finely chopped rhubarb

½ cup brown sugar

⅓ cup soft butter

⅓ cup sugar

1 egg

1½ cups flour

2 tsp baking powder

½ tsp salt

½ tsp nutmeg

½ cup milk

- Combine melted butter, rhubarb and brown sugar in small bowl and mix well.

- Spread evenly in greased muffin pans.

- Beat together butter, sugar and egg until fluffy.

- Combine flour, baking powder, salt and nutmeg and add to creamed mixture alternately with milk.

- Stir to just moisten, then spoon on top of rhubarb mixture.

- Bake at 190°C for 20–25 minutes.

- Invert on cooling rack and leave pan over muffins for a few minutes so all the rhubarb runs out. Serve warm.

Vanilla & Coconut Muffins

1 cup flour

1 cup coconut

1¾ tsp baking powder

3 tblsp brown sugar

2 tblsp butter, melted and
cooled slightly

½ cup milk

1 egg

½ tsp vanilla essence

coconut for sprinkling

ICING

2 cups icing sugar

1 tsp vanilla essence

1 tblsp butter

milk to mix

- In large bowl mix together flour, coconut, baking powder and brown sugar.

- In separate bowl mix together butter, milk, egg and vanilla.

- Make well in centre of dry ingredients and add milk mixture. Stir to just combine.

- Spoon batter into prepared muffin pans and bake at 190°C for 10–15 minutes.

- Top with vanilla icing and sprinkle with coconut.

- To make icing, mix ingredients together.

Vanilla Poppy Seed Muffins

150g butter
¾ cup sugar
1 egg, beaten
150g vanilla yoghurt
1 tsp vanilla essence
1½ cups flour
1 tsp baking powder
1 tsp baking soda
3 tblsp poppy seeds

- Cream butter and sugar, then stir in remaining ingredients until just combined.

- Spoon into muffin pans lined with paper cases and bake at 160°C for 15–20 minutes.

Vegetable & Ham Muffins

5 cups flour

1½ cups mixed vegetables

½ cup finely chopped bacon
or ham

2 cups grated cheese

50g butter, melted

5 tsp baking powder

salt

1 onion or chives, finely chopped

3 eggs, beaten

1 tsp vegetable stock powder

milk to mix

- Mix all ingredients together with milk to make a soft dough.

- Spoon into greased muffin pans.

- Bake at 200°C for about 20 minutes.

- Quantities can be halved.

Whiskey Raisin Muffins

1 cup raisins

¼ cup whiskey

2 tblsp honey

1 cup yoghurt

¼ cup milk

50g butter, melted

1 egg

2 cups flour

2 tsp baking powder

⅓ cup sugar

- Gently heat raisins and whiskey, then leave to soak for at least an hour.

- Add remaining ingredients to raisins and mix until just combined.

- Spoon into well-greased muffin pans and bake at 180°C for 15–20 minutes.

Wholemeal Spicy Pumpkin Muffins

½ cup packed brown sugar

¼ cup vegetable oil

1 egg

½ cup mashed cooked pumpkin

½ cup sultanas

1½ cups wholemeal
self-raising flour

½ tsp salt

¼ tsp nutmeg

¼ tsp mixed spice

½ cup milk (approx.)

• Beat together sugar, oil, egg
  and mashed pumpkin until
  well blended. Stir in sultanas.

• Sift flour, salt and spices.

• Stir into pumpkin mixture
  alternately with milk until just
  combined.

• Three-quarters fill greased
  muffin pans and bake at 200°C
  for 15–20 minutes.

Yoghurt & Sultana Muffins

1 cup plain flour

½ tsp baking powder

½ tsp salt

¼ tsp baking soda

¾ cup wheatgerm

4 tblsp packed brown sugar

1 egg, beaten

1 cup yoghurt

75g melted butter, cooled

½ cup sultanas

1 tblsp milk (optional)

- Sift flour, baking powder, salt and baking soda. Stir in wheatgerm and brown sugar.

- Combine beaten egg, yoghurt (adding milk if very thick) and cooled butter, and add to dry ingredients.

- Add sultanas and stir until just moistened. Do not over mix.

- Three-quarters fill greased muffin pans and bake at 190°C for 20–25 minutes.

Zucchini Muffins

1 egg	• Beat together egg, sugar, oil and buttermilk.
¼ cup sugar	
2 tblsp oil	• Combine dry ingredients.
½ cup buttermilk	• Add zucchini and wet ingredients to dry ingredients.
1¼ cups wholemeal flour	
1 tsp baking powder	• Mix until all ingredients are just combined, and spoon into prepared muffin pans.
½ tsp baking soda	
2–3 tsp ground cinnamon	
2 cups grated zucchini	• Bake in a preheated oven at 180°C for 20–30 minutes.

Zucchini Nut Muffins

3 cups flour

1 tsp baking powder

1 tsp baking soda

½ tsp salt

1 tsp cinnamon

2 cups sugar

4 eggs, room temperature

1 cup canola oil

2 cups grated zucchini

½ tsp vanilla essence

1 cup chopped walnuts

½ cup raisins

- Preheat oven to 180°C. Grease muffin pans.

- Sift dry ingredients (except sugar) and set aside.

- Combine sugar and eggs. Beat 2 minutes. Add oil and beat for 3 minutes.

- Add zucchini, vanilla, nuts and raisins.

- Fold in dry ingredients until mixed.

- Fill muffin pans two-thirds full and bake for 25 minutes.

- Wonderful with berry jam.

Zucchini Ricotta Muffins

1½ cups flour

2 tblsp sugar

3 tsp baking powder

½ tsp salt

¾ tsp dill

¼ cup milk

½ cup margarine or
butter, melted

2 large eggs

⅔ cup ricotta cheese

½ cup shredded zucchini

- In large bowl, combine flour, sugar, baking powder, salt and dill. Mix well.

- In medium bowl combine milk, margarine and eggs.

- Stir in ricotta cheese and zucchini and beat well.

- Add to dry ingredients, stirring until just moistened (batter will be stiff).

- Fill prepared muffin pans two-thirds full.

- Bake at 200°C for 20–25 minutes or until golden brown.

Index

PENGUIN BOOKS

Published by the Penguin Group
Penguin Group (Australia)
250 Camberwell Road, Camberwell, Victoria 3124, Australia
(a division of Pearson Australia Group Pty Ltd)
Penguin Group (USA) Inc.
375 Hudson Street, New York, New York 10014, USA
Penguin Group (Canada)
90 Eglinton Avenue East, Suite 700, Toronto ON M4P 2Y3, Canada
(a division of Pearson Penguin Canada Inc.)
Penguin Books Ltd
80 Strand, London WC2R 0RL, England
Penguin Ireland
25 St Stephen's Green, Dublin 2, Ireland
(a division of Penguin Books Ltd)
Penguin Books India Pvt Ltd
11 Community Centre, Panchsheel Park, New Delhi – 110 017, India
Penguin Group (NZ)
67 Apollo Drive, Rosedale, North Shore 0632, New Zealand
(a division of Pearson New Zealand Ltd)
Penguin Books (South Africa) (Pty) Ltd
24 Sturdee Avenue, Rosebank, Johannesburg 2196, South Africa

Penguin Books Ltd, Registered Offices: 80 Strand, London, WC2R 0RL, England

First published by Penguin Group (NZ) Ltd, 2001. This illustrated edition published by Penguin Group (Australia),
a division of Pearson Australia Group Pty Ltd, 2006

This edition published 2009 for Index Books Ltd

10 9 8 7 6

Text copyright © Penguin Group (NZ) Ltd, 2001
Design and photographs copyright © Penguin Group (Australia) 2006

The moral right of the author has been asserted

Many thanks go to photographer Julie Renouf, food stylist and muffin maker Julie Lanham, and Danielle Toigo
of Creative Homewares in Albert Park, Victoria, who provided a selection of the beautiful props.

Cover and text design by Elizabeth Theodosiadis © Penguin Group (Australia)
Cover photograph by Julie Renouf
Typeset by Post Pre-press Group, Brisbane, Queensland
Printed in China by SNP Leefung Printing Co. Ltd

National Library of Australia
Cataloguing-in-Publication data:

  Muffin Bible.
  Includes index.
  ISBN 978 0 14 104600 6.
  1. Muffins.

  641.8157

penguin.com.au
penguin.co.nz